FRAs and Interest-Rate Futures

FRAs AND INTEREST-RATE FUTURES

Brian Coyle

FINANCIAL
WORLD
Publishing
THE CHARTERED INSTITUTE OF BANKERS

Financial World Publishing
IFS House
4-9 Burgate Lane
Canterbury
Kent
CT1 2XJ
United Kingdom

Telephone: 01227 818687

Financial World Publishing publications are published by
The Chartered Institute of Bankers, a non-profit making registered educational charity.

Typeset by Kevin O'Connor
Printed in Italy

ISBN 0-85297-444-2

Contents

What are FRAs?

A forward-rate agreement or FRA is a financial instrument that can be used to fix the rate of interest on a short-term loan or deposit starting at a date some time in the future.

It is a contract relating to the level of short-term interest rates, as defined by an agreed benchmark rate of interest, for example three-month LIBOR, at a specified time in the future. An FRA is not an actual short-term loan or deposit. The interest rate fixed by the FRA is on an agreed notional amount of principal, rather than an actual loan or deposit.

FRAs are bought and sold. Banks that trade FRAs will quote prices for both buying and selling.

- The buyer of an FRA obtains a fixed rate of interest for payment.
- The seller of an FRA obtains a fixed rate of interest to receive.

The parties to an FRA agreement typically are two banks, but might be a bank and a corporate customer.

Purpose of FRAs

An FRA can be used to manage short-term interest-rate risk. An organization that is concerned about the risk of a rise or fall in short-term interest rates in the near future can buy or sell FRAs to hedge the risk.

FRAs therefore are likely to be more useful when the general level of interest rates in the money markets is volatile.

Because an FRA locks in an interest rate today for a future loan or deposit period, it can be used by:

- a borrower who will be paying variable-rate interest on a future loan, who wants to fix the cost of the borrowing now and so avoid the risk of a rise in interest rates by the time the actual loan period begins
- an investor who will be receiving variable-rate interest on a future short-term deposit, who wants to fix the rate of interest receivable now and so avoid the risk of a fall in interest rates before the actual deposit period begins.

How an FRA Works

An FRA is an agreement relating to the rate of interest on a notional amount of principal for an agreed future lending period. It is similar in some respects to an interest-rate swap.

- One party to the agreement, the buyer of the FRA, agrees to pay a fixed rate of interest on the notional loan/deposit. This fixed rate is specified in the agreement. In return, the buyer will receive interest at the current market rate of interest prevailing at the start of the notional loan/deposit period.
- The other party, the seller, agrees to pay interest on the notional loan/deposit at the current market rate at the start of the loan/ deposit period, and to receive in return the fixed rate of interest specified in the agreement.

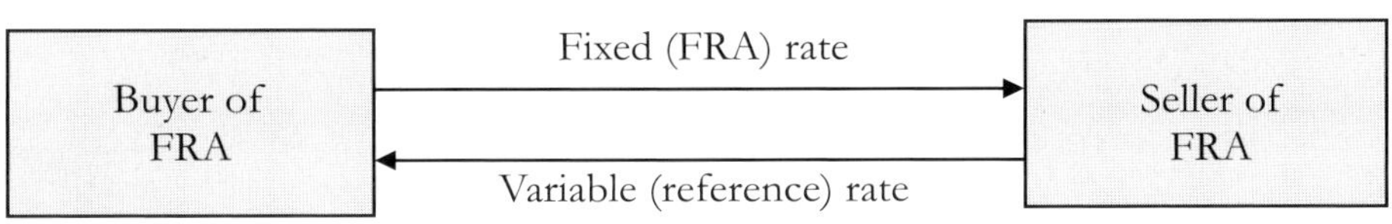

An FRA contract is settled at the start of the notional loan/deposit period. Because the buyer and seller have agreed to exchange interest payments on the notional principal, in practise there is simply a single net payment by one party to the other.

- If the current rate of interest is higher than the fixed rate specified in the FRA, there will be a net payment from the buyer to the seller.
- If the current interest rate is lower than the fixed rate specified in the FRA, there will be a net payment from the seller to the buyer.

This net payment, or **compensation payment**, is based on the difference between the current interest rate and the fixed rate in the FRA agreement, and it is based on the amount of notional principal and the length of the notional loan/deposit period. The calculation of the compensation payment is explained later.

The Reference Rate

The compensation payment is based on the difference between the fixed interest rate in the FRA and what the current market rate of interest proves to be at the start of the notional loan/deposit period.

This current market rate of interest, known as the reference rate or settlement rate, is an agreed benchmark rate of interest for the appropriate term of the notional loan/deposit. For example, if the notional loan period is three months and the notional principal amount is in sterling, the reference rate will be the three-month sterling London Inter Bank Offered Rate (LIBOR).

The date for fixing the reference rate typically is two working days before the settlement date for the contract. This gives time for one party to the FRA to arrange for the compensation payment to be made to the other party on settlement date.

Key Dates in an FRA Agreement

There are four key dates in an FRA agreement.

- Contract date, the date on which the FRA agreement is made.
- The start date for the notional loan/interest rate period, also the date on which the contract is settled. This is known as value date, spot date or settlement date.
- Fixing date, the date on which the reference rate is fixed for the purpose of settling the contract on settlement date. Typically this is two working days before settlement date.
- Maturity date, the final date of the notional loan/deposit period. The notional loan/deposit period therefore runs from settlement date to maturity date.

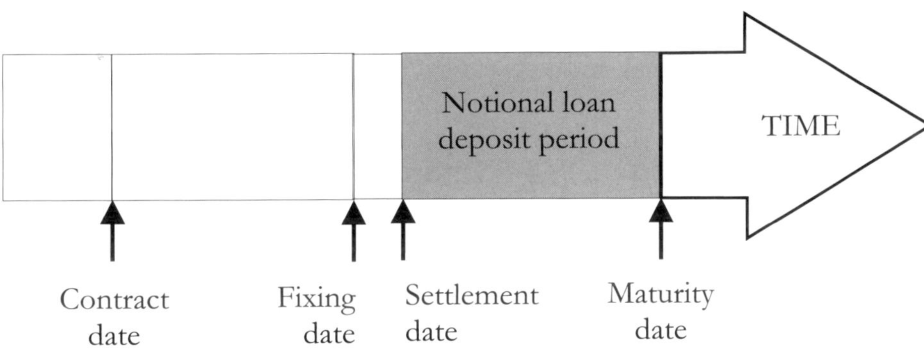

Notional Principal

An FRA is an agreement relating to the level of interest rate on a loan or deposit of a given term, but it is not an agreement to lend or invest an amount of capital. The only payment is the compensation payment based on the difference in interest rates at fixing date. The agreement therefore is based on a notional amount of principal.

Terms of an FRA

An FRA is a binding contract on both parties that must specify:

- the identities of both the buyer and the seller of the FRA
- the currency and amount of notional principal
- the date from which the notional loan/deposit period begins, that is also settlement date
- either the maturity date or the term of the notional loan/deposit period
- the fixed rate of interest payable by the buyer of the FRA and receivable by the seller of the FRA
- the reference rate against which the compensation amount will be paid at settlement, e.g. LIBOR for the appropriate maturity.

Because an FRA is an over-the-counter instrument, its terms can be tailored to the specific requirements of the customer. Typically, however, most FRAs are for notional loan/deposit periods of three, six, nine or twelve months.

Example

A corporation expects to have a requirement to borrow £20 million in two months. The loan period will be three months. The corporation's treasurer is concerned about the current volatility in three-month LIBOR rates, and wishes to hedge the interest-rate risk using an FRA.

The risk is that three-month LIBOR will rise by the time the loan period begins, and the corporation's treasurer wishes to fix an interest rate for the future loan.

He can do this by arranging to buy an FRA from a bank. It would buy an FRA on a notional principal amount of £20 million, for a period starting at the end of two months and with a term of three months (to the end of month 5). The reference rate for the FRA will be three-month sterling LIBOR.

Suppose the FRA bank quotes a fixed rate of 6.25%. Suppose also that the contract date is Friday 12 May, settlement date is Wednesday 12 July and fixing date is Monday 10 July.

- If, on fixing date, three-month LIBOR is above 6.25%, the FRA bank will make a compensation payment to the corporation on settlement date, in settlement of the contract. The compensation payment will be based on the difference between the fixed rate of 6.25% and the three-month LIBOR rate on fixing date.
- If, on fixing date, three-month LIBOR is below 6.25%, the corporation will make a compensation payment to the FRA bank on settlement date, in settlement of the contract. The compensation payment will be based on the difference between the fixed rate of 6.25% and the three-month LIBOR rate on fixing date.

Who Makes the Payment on Settlement Date?

	FRA bank sells the FRA. Customer buys the FRA	*FRA bank buys the FRA Customer buys the FRA*
Reference rate higher than fixed FRA rate	FRA banks pays the customer	Customer pays the FRA bank
Reference rate lower than fixed FRA rate	Customer pays the FRA bank	FRA bank pays the customer

Buyer of an FRA: Fixing a Borrowing Rate

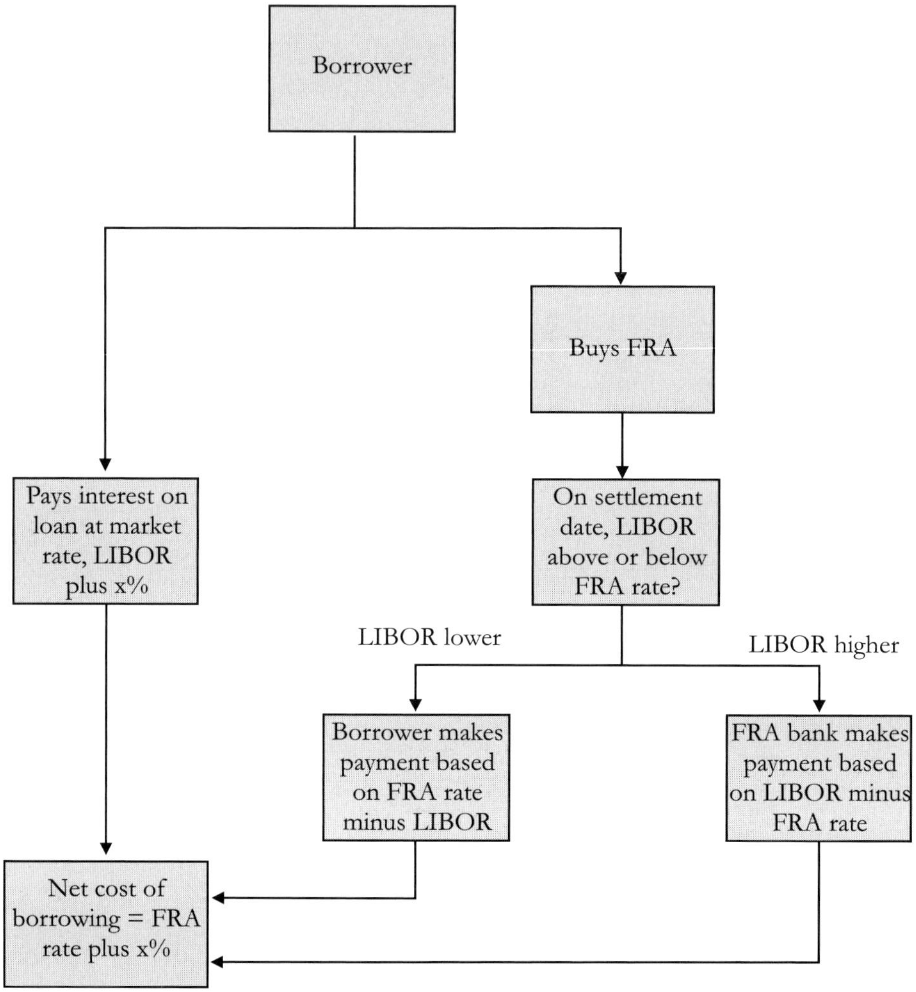

Seller of an FRA: Fixing a Lending or Investing Rate

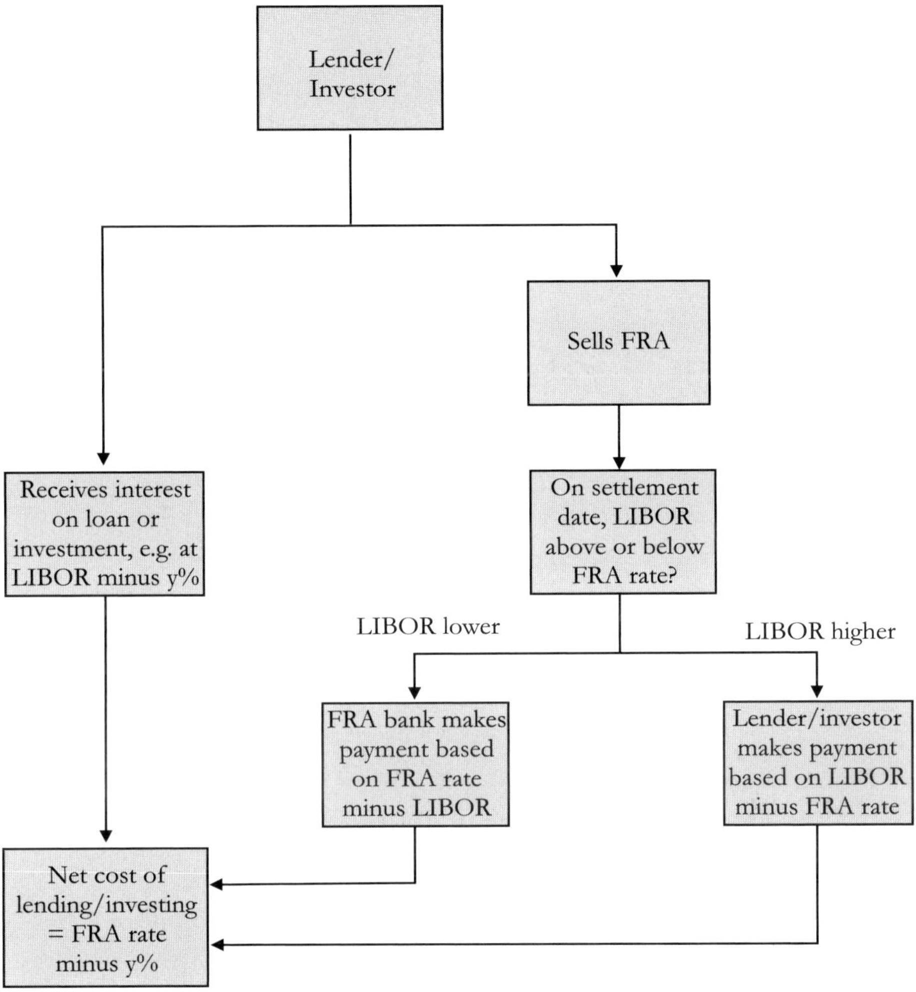

How Does an FRA Hedge an Exposure to Interest-Rate Risk?

An FRA can be used to hedge interest-rate risk because the compensation payment offsets the movement in market interest rates. If market interest rates move adversely, there should be a compensation payment receivable from the FRA. If market interest rates move favorably, the benefit will be offset by having to make a compensation payment with the FRA. The net effect is to fix the hedger's interest rate at a rate determined when the FRA agreement was made.

Example

In the previous example, a corporation bought an FRA because it wished to hedge the risk of a rise in three-month LIBOR.

It bought an FRA at 6.25% on £20 million for a notional loan period starting at the end of month 2 and ending at the end of month 5.

Suppose the corporation can borrow at three-month LIBOR plus 50 basis points (0.5%). The FRA therefore should fix the corporation's borrowing rate at 6.25% plus 50 basis points, i.e. at 6.75%.

Suppose first of all that at fixing date, actual three-month LIBOR is 7.25%. The corporation will borrow £20 million at LIBOR plus 50 basis points, i.e. at 7.75%. However, the corporation will receive a compensation payment from the FRA equivalent to the difference between the fixed rate in the FRA (6.25%) and the reference rate at fixing date (7.25%).

	%
Corporation borrows at LIBOR plus 50 bp	7.75
Compensation from FRA, equivalent to	1.00
Net borrowing cost fixed at	6.75

Suppose instead that at fixing date, actual three-month LIBOR is 5.0%. The corporation will borrow £20 million at LIBOR plus 50 basis points, i.e. at 5.50%. However, the corporation will have to make a compensation payment to the FRA equivalent to the difference between the fixed rate in the FRA (6.25%) and the reference rate at fixing date (5.0%).

	%
Corporation borrows at LIBOR plus 50 bp	5.50
Compensation payment payable, equivalent to	1.25
Net borrowing cost fixed at	6.75

Buying and Selling Terminology

The buyer of an FRA might express the agreement in terms such as:

- 'We buy 6.52% on $30 million for six against nine months', or
- 'We buy 6.52% on $30 million for 6 v 9.'

Here, the buyer is agreeing to pay 6.52% on notional principal of $30 million, for a notional loan period of three months, staring at the end of month 6 and ending at the end of month 9. Settlement date will be at the end of month 6. The buyer will receive in return interest on the same notional principal, determined on fixing date with reference to a benchmark rate, such as three-month dollar LIBOR.

Similar terminology applies to selling FRAs. For example:

'We sell 5.88% on £40 million for 3 v 12'.

The terminology for FRAs is not standardized, and there are different ways of describing the notional loan/deposit period. All the terms listed below could be used to describe an FRA with a notional loan/deposit period starting at the end of month 3 (settlement date) and ending at the end of month 6 (maturity date):

- 3 v 6
- three against six months
- threes, sixes
- three on six
- three by six
- three over sixes.

Because FRAs are over-the-counter instruments, they can be tailored to the specific requirements of a customer. However, common FRA periods are:

1 v 3
1 v 6
2 v 5
2 v 6

3 v 6
3 v 9
3 v 12
6 v 12
6 v 18
9 v 12
9 v 15
9 v 18
12 v 18
12 v 24.

FRA Prices

Banks trading FRAs quote two-way prices, a bid rate and an offer rate, for the fixed rate for each notional loan/deposit term.

- The bid rate is the fixed rate that the bank will want to receive in exchange for paying out at the reference rate.
- The offer rate is the fixed rate that the bank will pay out in exchange for receiving interest at the reference rate.

No premium or commission is payable to the FRA bank for entering an FRA agreement, and the bank seeks to make its profit from the difference between the bid and offer rates. The bid rate will be higher than the offer rate because the FRA bank will wish to receive a higher fixed rate than it pays out.

Example
A bank trading FRAs might quote prices for FRAs in dollars as follows: (the figures are illustrative).

	$
3 v 6	5.83-5.79
4 v 7	5.89-5.85
5 v 8	5.98-5.93
6 v 9	6.12-6.06
9 v 12	6.24-6.17
3 v 9	5.92-5.88
4 v 10	6.02-5.97
5 v 11	6.10-6.05
6 v 12	6.19-6.13

In this example, the first five prices are for FRAs with three-month notional loan periods and the next four are for FRAs with six-month periods. The higher bid rate is quoted first.

Screen-based prices are indicative only, and not all maturities are quoted. A counterparty seeking a rate quotation for an FRA would have to telephone a bank or broker and ask for a quotation specific to its requirements.

Summary: Buying and Selling Terminology

Customer buys FRA
Bank sells FRA
Bank receives the fixed rate and pays the variable (reference) rate
Bank quotes the (higher) bid rate.
Customer sells FRA
Bank buys FRA
Bank pays the fixed rate and receives the variable (reference) rate
Bank quotes the (lower) offer rate

The Amount of the Compensation Payment

The compensation payment on settlement of an FRA is based on the difference between the fixed rate in the agreement and the reference rate as at fixing date, applied to the notional principal amount and the term of the notional loan/deposit.

For example, suppose that for a 2v6 FRA on notional principal of £30 million, the fixed rate is 7.00% and that on fixing date four-month LIBOR is 7.25%. The compensation payment should be based on the difference between the two rates, 0.25%, applied to a principal amount of £30 million for a four-month term.

The payment will not be exactly this amount, however. This is because interest on a short-term loan accrues through the loan period and becomes payable only at the end of the period. Similarly, interest on a short-term deposit accrues through the period, and is receivable at the end of the period. In contrast, the settlement of an FRA takes place at the very beginning of the notional loan/deposit period.

To allow for the fact that the compensation payment is made at the start of the period, and not at the end of it, the amount payable is adjusted downwards. It is discounted to a present value, from an end-of-period value to a start-of-period value.

Example
A bank sells a 3 v 9 FRA to a customer on notional principal of $25 million. The fixed rate is 6.50%.

On fixing date six-month dollar LIBOR is 6.10%.

At settlement, the bank will receive a compensation payment as seller of the FRA, because the fixed rate (receivable) is higher than the variable rate (payable). The amount of the payment receivable should be based on interest of 0.4% p.a. (6.50% - 6.10%) on principal of $25 million for a term of (9 – 3) six months.

However, the amount of interest is discounted, because the compensation payment will be made on settlement date instead of at the end of a further six months. The discount rate applied is the reference rate, that in this case would be the six-month dollar LIBOR rate, 6.10%.

The compensation payment formula

The formula for calculating the compensation payment is as follows:

$$P \times (R - F) \times \frac{D}{Y} \times \left[\frac{1}{1 + \frac{(R \times D)}{Y}}\right]$$

Explanation of the Formula

The formula has four elements.

- P is the notional principal amount.
- (R – F) is the difference between the reference rate on fixing date and the fixed rate in the FRA agreement. R is the reference rate for the FRA agreement, e.g. three-month LIBOR or six-month LIBOR. It is expressed as a percentage value or as a proportion (e.g. 7% or 0.07) and not as a whole number (e.g. not 7). F is the fixed rate, and is also expressed as a percentage amount or as a proportion, not as a whole number.
- D/Y is a statement of the term of the notional loan/deposit period, as a fraction of a full year. FRAs use money-market interest conventions. D is the actual length of the notional loan/deposit period in days. Y is the number of interest-earning days in the year according to money-market interest conventions. For most currencies, including the dollar and the euro, this is 360. For some currencies, such as sterling, it is 365.
- The fourth element in the formula is the discount factor. This reduces the interest payable or receivable to a present value as at settlement date.

If R exceeds F, the compensation payment goes from the seller of the FRA to the buyer.

If R is lower than F, the compensation payment that will be a negative amount if the formula above is applied, goes from the buyer of the FRA to the seller.

Example 1

A company has a variable-rate loan of £20 million. It pays interest every six months, at a rate of LIBOR plus 100 basis points, i.e. LIBOR plus 1%. The next interest payment is due in six months. The company's finance director is worried about the risk of a rise in six-month LIBOR and decides to hedge the next interest payment. The company therefore buys a 6 v 12 FRA on £20 million. The fixed rate is 6.20%.

On fixing date six months later, six-month LIBOR is 7.50%.

The company therefore will receive a compensation payment from the FRA bank. Assuming that the length of the notional interest period is for example 182 days, the size of the payment will be:

$$£20 \text{ million x } (7.50\% - 6.20\%) \text{ x } 182/365 \text{ x } \frac{1}{\left[1 + \frac{(0.075 \text{ x } 182)}{365}\right]}$$

= £124,970.29

The interest rate payable on the company's loan for the six-month period will be LIBOR plus 1%, that is 8.50% assuming that the LIBOR rate is still 7.50% on the rollover date for the loan. The company therefore will pay interest at 8.50% for six months, but will receive compensation of £124,970.29 at the start of the six-month period. The net result is that the effective borrowing cost for the six-month period will be 7.20%, the rate fixed by the FRA (6.20%) plus the 100 basis points that the company pays above LIBOR on its loan.

Example 2

Another company expects to receive $30 million two months from now that it will put on deposit for three months with a London-based bank. The company expects to receive interest at LIBOR minus 50 basis points.

It wants to hedge the risk of a fall in LIBOR over the next two months, and therefore arranges to sell a 2 v 5 FRA on $30 million. The fixed rate in the FRA is, for example, 5.90%.

Two months later, on fixing date, three-month LIBOR is 6.80%

The company therefore will make a compensation payment to the FRA bank. Assuming that the length of the notional interest period is, for example 92 days, the size of the payment will be:

$$\$30 \text{ million} \times (6.80\ \% - 5.90\ \%) \times 92/360 \times \frac{1}{\left[1 + \frac{(0.068 \times 92)}{360}\right]}$$

= $67,821.41

Note
The money-market convention is for a 360-day year for most currencies, including the dollar.

The interest rate receivable by the company on its three-month deposit will be LIBOR minus 0.5%, 6.30% assuming that the LIBOR rate is still 6.80 % on the rollover date for the loan. The company therefore will receive interest at 6.30% for three months, but will receive compensation of $67,821.41 at the start of the three-month period. The net result is that the effective interest yield for the three-month period will be just 5.40 %, the rate fixed by the FRA (5.90 %) minus the 50 basis points below LIBOR receivable on the company's deposit.

FRAs, Interest-Rate Swaps and Interest-Rate Futures

An FRA is similar to an interest-rate coupon swap, in the sense that it is an agreement between two parties to exchange an interest-rate payment on a notional amount of principal at a future date. One party to the agreement pays a fixed rate of interest, agreed when the contract is made. The other party pays a variable rate of interest, determined by a benchmark rate of interest at a future fixing date.

An FRA involves just one exchange of interest payments. A coupon swap involves a series of payments at intervals over the term of the swap, and is a longer-term instrument.

FRAs also are similar to interest-rate futures, in the sense that they are contracts fixing the short-term rate of interest on a notional amount of principal. Whereas FRAs are over-the-counter instruments that can be tailored to the client's specific requirements, futures are standardized exchange-traded instruments offering considerable flexibility and liquidity to their users.

Banks trading FRAs might hedge the exposures arising on their FRA positions by taking an offsetting position in interest-rate futures. For example, if a bank sells FRAs on $50 million and so is exposed to the risk of a rise in short-term dollar interest rates, it might decide to hedge the risk by selling dollar interest-rate futures.

Summary

A forward-rate agreement is an over-the-counter derivative instrument, in which one party (the buyer) agrees to pay interest at a fixed rate in exchange for interest at a variable rate, on a notional amount of principal for an agreed term starting at a date in the future. The other party (the seller) undertakes to receive interest at a fixed rate in exchange for paying interest at a variable rate.

The variable rate subsequently is fixed just before settlement date by reference to a benchmark rate of interest such as LIBOR.

FRAs can be used:

1) to hedge the risk of adverse interest-rate movements in the fairly near future
2) by arbitrageurs and speculators, seeking to profit from unexpected short-term interest-rate movements or from the mispricing of FRAs against other financial instruments.

FRAs can be negotiated for a variety of notional loan/interest periods, ranging from a few weeks to several years. However, most FRAs are for notional loan/deposit periods of less than a year, and so FRAs generally are regarded as money-market instruments.

FRAs are agreements based on a notional amount of principal. No principal is exchanged between buyer and seller. The only payment is a compensation payment by one party to the other on settlement date.

The amount of the compensation payment is the interest value of the difference between the fixed rate of interest in the agreement and the reference rate of interest on fixing date, discounted to a present value to allow for the fact that settlement occurs at the start of the notional loan/deposit period, not at the end.

FRAs are similar in many respects to both interest-rate coupon swaps and interest-rate futures.

FRA Rates

How are FRA Rates Determined?

FRA rates are derived from current spot rates in the interbank market, and are based on forward/forward rates that make up a forward yield curve.

A forward/forward rate is an interest rate for a loan or deposit starting at a future date. An example of a forward/forward rate would be the three-month sterling interest rate for a loan/deposit period starting two months from now and ending five months from now.

A forward/forward rate is derived from two spot interbank market rates. For example, the forward/forward three-month sterling rate for a loan period starting two months from now can be derived from the spot two-month and the spot five-month LIBOR rates.

Deriving a Forward/Forward Rate

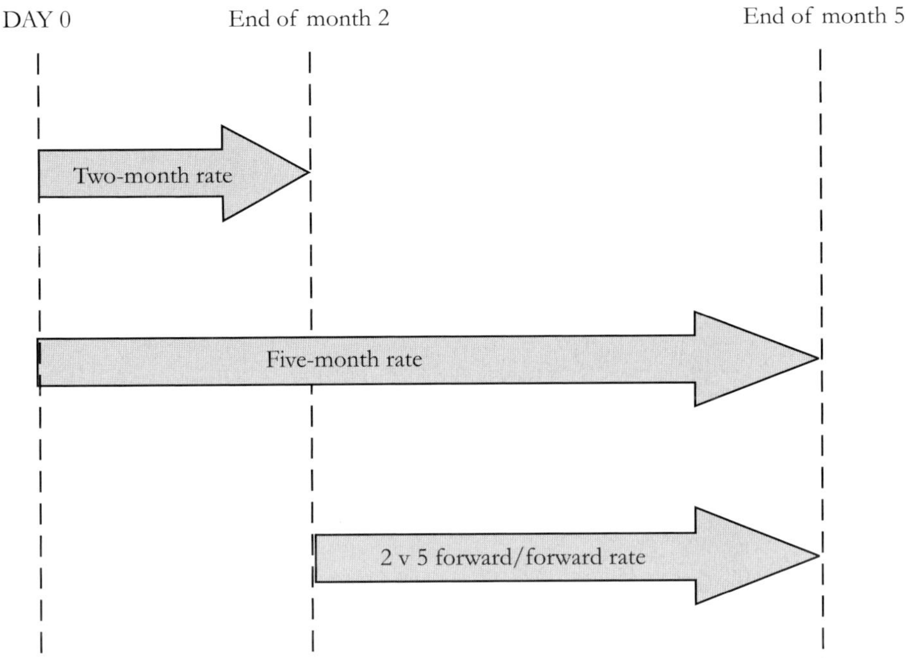

Deriving a Forward/Forward Rate

The calculation of forward/forward rates is a routine computerized procedure, but it might help to illustrate the technique with an example.

Example
The current three-month euribor rate (the benchmark money-market interest rate for the euro) is 4.5% per annum and the one-year euribor rate is 5.0%

So what is the 3 v 12 forward/forward rate for the euro, derived from these two spot euribor rates?

It will be assumed that the next three-month period has 92 days.

Note

The money market for the euro is based on an actual/360-day interest convention. This means that the interest accrued in any period is calculated as:

$$\text{Principal} \times \text{Interest rate p.a.} \times \frac{\text{Actual calendar days in the interest period}}{360}$$

Analysis

The 3 v 12 forward/forward rate can be derived from the spot rates for three months and one year.

1. At the current spot rate, €1,000 could be lent now for the next three months to earn interest of €11.50 by the end of the period.

   €1,000 x 4.5% x 92/360 = €11.50.

   This means that by the end of month 3, the original €1,000 will have increased in value, with interest, to €1,011.50.

2. Similarly, at the current spot rate, €1,000 could be lent now for the next twelve months to earn interest of €50.69 by the end of the period.

   €1,000 x 5% x 365/360 = €50.69.

   This means that by the end of month 12, the original €1,000 will have increased in value, with interest, to €1,050.69.

3. Banks currently are willing to lend at either 4.5% for three months or 5% for 12 months. It follows that in the current market, €1,011.50 by the end of month 3, and €1,050.69 by the end of month 12 have an equal value.

   The 3 v 12 forward/forward rate therefore can be calculated as the interest rate at which €1,011.50 lent at the end of month 3 would become €1,050.69, with accrued interest, by the end of month 12.

   Therefore we need to calculate the interest rate at which

€1,011.50 lent for 273 days (365 days – 92 days) will earn interest of €39.19 (1,050.69 – 1,011.50).

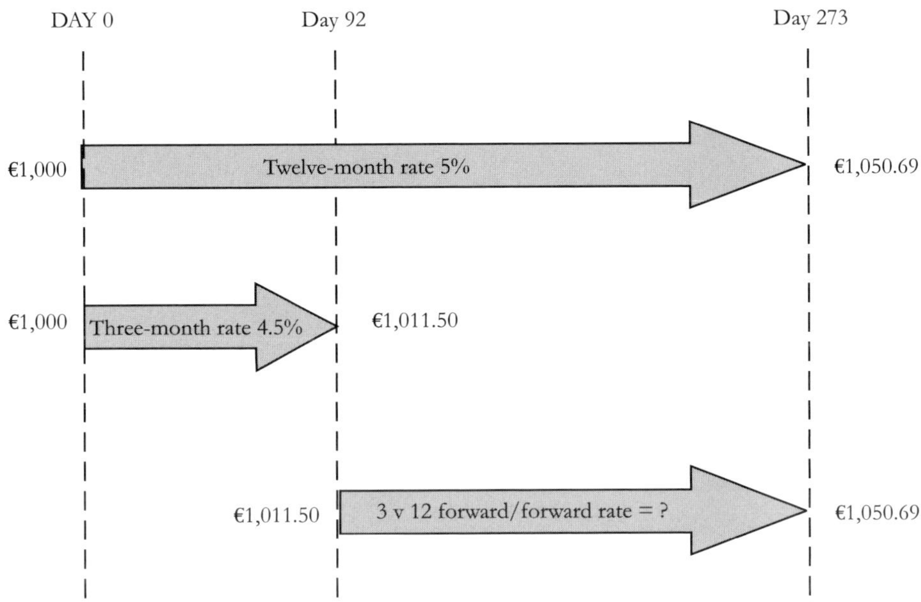

4. Interest is calculated as follows:
   P x R x D/Y = I
   Where:
   - P is the principal amount
   - R is the interest rate, per annum
   - D is the actual number of days in the interest period
   - Y is the day base convention for the number of days in the year, for the euro 360.
   - I is the amount of interest earned.

   Re-arranging this formula, we get:

   R = (I/P) x (Y/D)

5. Applying this formula to the example, we get:

   R = (€39.19/€1,011.50) x (360/273)

R = 0.0511, i.e. 5.11% per annum

The 3 v 12 forward/forward rate therefore is 5.11%.

6. A bank can quote a 3 v 12 FRA rate based on 5.11% per annum. This is because, ignoring the spread between a bank's borrowing and lending rates, and assuming that the bank can both borrow and lend at the euribor rate, the same earnings can be achieved by either:

- Lending euros now for 12 months at 5%, and
- Lending euros now for 3 months at 4.5% and simultaneously selling a 3 v 12 FRA at 5.11%.

Forward/Forward-Rate Formula

A formula for calculating a forward/forward rate is as follows:

$$\left[\frac{1+\left(LR \times \frac{LT}{Y}\right)}{1+\left(SR \times \frac{ST}{Y}\right)} - 1\right] \times \frac{Y}{LT - ST)}$$

Where:

LR is the spot market rate for the interest period with the longer maturity

SR is the spot market rate for the interest rate with the shorter maturity

LT is the number of days in the interest period with the longer maturity

ST is the number of days in the interest period with the shorter maturity

Y is the day-base convention, 360 for most currencies, but 365 for some currencies, including sterling.

In the previous example, the 3 v12 forward/forward rate could have been calculated as follows:

$$\left[\frac{1+\left(0.05 \times \frac{365}{360}\right)}{1+\left(0.045 \times \frac{92}{360}\right)} - 1\right] \times \frac{360}{(365-92)}$$

= 5.11

Exercise

What is the 2 v 5 forward/forward rate for sterling, if the two-month LIBOR rate is 6.375% and the five-month LIBOR rate is 6.5%?

Assume that the two-month interest period has 61 days and the five-month period has 153 days.

The sterling money markets have a day-base convention of actual/365.

Solution

LR = .065
SR = .06375
LT = 153 days
ST = 92 days
D = 365

The forward/forward rate is:

$$\left[\frac{1+\left(0.065 \times \frac{153}{365}\right)}{1+\left(0.06375 \times \frac{92}{365}\right)} - 1\right] \times \frac{365}{(153-92)}$$

=

$$\left[\frac{1.02724658}{1.01606849} - 1\right] \times \frac{365}{61}$$

= 6.58

The 2 v 5 forward/forward rate is 6.58%.

The Bid/Offer Spread

Indicative rates displayed by banks trading FRAs show a typical spread between its bid and offer rates of about 0.05% - 0.10% (5 to 10 basis points).

Because of the spread between a bank's borrowing and lending rates in the interbank market, e.g. the spread between LIBOR and LIBID, there should be in principle a wider spread between FRA bid and offer rates.

In practise, market forces push rates to a smaller spread around the central rate, i.e. the average of the bank's borrowing and lending rates, LIMEAN.

For example, suppose that the following spot rates apply for the dollar:

Term	$ LIBOR	$ LIBID	LIMEAN
3 months	6.50%	6.375%	6.4375%
9 months	6.75%	6.625%	6.6875%

Assuming that there are 92 days in the three-month interest period and 276 days in the nine-month period, the 3 v 9 forward/forward rate would be 6.72%. A bank therefore might quote 3 v 9 FRA rates for the dollar of about 6.74%-6.70%.

Forward Yield Curves

A yield curve shows the interest rates for interest periods of different maturities, for example the spot LIBOR rate for maturities of one week, one month, two months, three months, and so on.

A forward yield curve shows forward/forward interest rates for interest periods of different maturities. Each forward yield curve has one start date. For example, a sterling LIBOR forward yield curve could be drawn from forward/forward rates such as the 2 v 3, 2 v 4, 2 v 5, 2 v 6 etc. rates.

Forward yield curves can be used to analyze the expected movements in the level of interest rates that have been factored into current spot rates.

Using FRAs

Who Uses FRAs?

FRAs are transacted in all freely traded currencies, particularly in dollars, euros, yen, Swiss francs and sterling. London is the main dealing center.

Transactions typically are for nominal principal amounts in the range $10 million-$100 million, but can be for larger or smaller amounts. Transaction sizes tend to be smaller for less-liquid currencies.

Most transactions are between banks, because FRAs are instruments for hedging short-term interest-rate risk, and financial institutions have greater exposures to this type of risk than most non-bank trading organizations. However, large companies also might use FRAs.

Why Use FRAs?

Like other interest-rate derivative instruments, FRAs are likely to be used more extensively when interest rates are volatile and there is uncertainty about the direction and size of future movements in interest rates.

FRAs might be used for several reasons:

- A bank or other organization with variable-rate borrowing, or which expects to have to borrow short-term in the future, can buy FRAs to hedge its exposures to the risk of a rise in interest rates. Buying FRAs locks in an effective borrowing cost.
- A bank or other organization with variable-rate investments, or which expects to make short-term investments in the future, can sell FRAs to hedge its exposures to the risk of a fall in

interest rates. Selling FRAs locks in an effective investment yield.

- Banks with a mismatch between short-term lending and borrowing can use FRAs to hedge their exposures to an unfavorable movement (up or down) in interest rates.
- Very occasionally, an opportunity for arbitrage might arise from the mispricing of FRAs by a bank. An organization can take advantage to secure a profit by buying or selling the mispriced FRAs.
- Conceivably, an organization might use FRAs to speculate by buying or selling FRAs, hoping to make a profit from a favorable movement in interest rates between contract date and settlement date.

Advantages and disadvantages of FRAs

Advantages	Disadvantages
FRAs are over-the-counter instruments and so can be tailored to the specific requirements of a customer.	Over-the-counter instruments are not tradable.
No front-end fee is payable.	Unlike interest-rate options (for the buyer of options) FRAs are binding agreements that must be settled at settlement date.
Nothing is payable or receivable until settlement date.	FRAs normally are more expensive than comparable interest-rate futures contracts. Futures might be preferred when tailor-made agreements are not necessary.
No borrowing or lending of capital is involved.	

The main advantage of FRAs over interest-rate futures is that they can be tailored to the customer's specific requirements, in particular with respect to the notional principal amount, currency and settlement date.

Hedging an Exposure to the Risk of a Rise in Interest Rates

An organization with variable-rate borrowings, or which expects to make short-term or variable-rate borrowing in the future, can hedge its exposure to the risk of a rise in interest rates between contract date and a future fixing date or rollover date for the loan.

Example
An organization has a $25 million loan at a floating rate of interest. Interest rates are reset every six months and the next resetting date is in six months' time.

The organization pays interest at dollar LIBOR plus 50 basis points. For the current six-month period just started, it will be paying 6.25% per annum.

The company does not want its borrowing costs in any six-month period to rise above 7%, but it is concerned about the risk of rising interest rates during the next few months.

It therefore considers buying a 6 v 12 FRA to hedge its exposure to the risk of higher interest rates six months from now by fixing the effective cost of the loan for the next six-month interest period.

Current spot rates for dollar LIBOR are:

6-month rate:	5.75%
12-month rate:	5.81%

An FRA bank quotes a bid price of 6.47% for a 6 v 12 FRA on $25 million.

Analysis

Because the organization is borrowing at LIBOR plus 50 basis points, an FRA rate of 6.47% allows it to lock in an effective borrowing cost of 6.97% for the 6 v 12 interest period: this is just within the maximum borrowing cost targeted by the organization.

Suppose for example that interest rates were to rise, and that on settlement date for the FRA that is timed to coincide with the date for resetting the rate of interest on the loan, the spot six-month LIBOR rate is 7.25 %. The organization's borrowing cost for the next six months will be 7.75% (LIBOR plus 50 bp).

The organization would receive a compensation payment from the FRA bank, based on the difference of 0.78% between the FRA rate of 6.47% and the reference interest rate of 7.25%.

Cost of borrowing (interest payable at end of six-month interest period)	7.75%
Compensation payment (receivable at beginning of six-month interest period)	0.78%
Effective borrowing cost	6.97%

A drawback to buying an FRA to hedge the exposure to a rise in borrowing costs is that the FRA fixes the borrowing cost. This means that if interest rates were to fall between contract date and settlement date, the organization could not benefit from the lower borrowing costs available in the market.

Strip of FRAs

An organization might have a variable-rate loan with regular rollover dates. It can hedge the exposure to the risk of higher interest rates at each rollover date by purchasing a strip of FRAs.

A strip of FRAs is a series of FRAs purchased or sold at the same contract date, for a succession of future interest periods.

For example, suppose that an organization has a variable-rate loan of E50 million, and the interest rate on the loan is reset every three months. The organization might decide to use FRAs to fix its borrowing costs for the next two years. To do so, it would buy a strip of FRAs, as follows:

FRA
3 v 6
6 v 9
9 v 12
12 v 15
15 v 18
18 v 21
21 v 24

Each FRA would lock in a different borrowing cost for each interest period, depending on the FRA rates available at contract date.

Hedging an Exposure to the Risk of a Fall in Interest Rates
An organization with variable-rate investments, or which expects to be making short-term investments in the future, can sell an FRA to hedge its exposure to the risk of falling interest rates between now and a future interest-fixing date.

Example
An organization expects to receive £10 million in three months' time, and plans to invest the money for a six-month period in money-market investments. It is concerned about the possibility that interest rates might fall sharply during the next three months.

It can hedge its exposure to the risk of a fall in interest rates by selling a 3 v 9 FRA on £10 million. This will lock in an effective income yield, based on the offer rate obtained for the FRA.

Mismatches Between Borrowing and Lending
A bank might use an FRA to hedge the interest-rate risk arising from a mismatch between its short-term borrowing and lending positions.

Example
A bank has borrowed \$60 million for three months at 5.50%. It has lent \$60 million for one month at 5.60%, expecting to relend the money for a further two months afterwards.

This creates an exposure to the risk of a fall in interest rates between now and the end of month 1, when the bank will relend the \$60 million plus accumulated interest earned on the one-month loan. It will want, at the very least, sufficient money at the end of month 3 to repay its borrowing with interest.

Suppose the one-month lending period has 31 days and that there are 91 days in the three-month period.

- The interest payable on the three-month loan will be \$60 million x 5.5% x 91/360 = \$834,166.67.
- The interest receivable on the one-month loan will be \$60 million x 5.60% x 31/360 = \$280,000.00.

The bank will require further interest income of \$554,166.67 (834,166.67 – 280,000) just to be able to repay its own three-month loan with interest. The money available for lending at the end of month 1 will be \$60,280,000.

The minimum interest yield required between month 1 and month 3, an interest period of 60 days, is therefore:

R = (554,166.67/60,280,000) x (360/61) = 5.43 %.

The bank can seek a quotation for selling a 1 v 3 FRA on \$60,280,000. Any rate in excess of 5.43% would lock in a profit on the borrowing and lending transactions overall.

Arbitrage Opportunities

Arbitrage involves taking advantage of pricing differences between related instruments or markets that offer the opportunity to secure an immediate and certain profit. Arbitrage opportunities, should they arise, ought to disappear very quickly as prices in the market are adjusted and re-aligned to eliminate the mispricing.

Example
A bank can borrow euros at the euribor rate. Three-month euribor currently is 4.25%.

The bank can invest funds for one month at the euribor rate of 4.12%.

It has an opportunity to sell a 1 v 3 FRA at 4.32%.

The three-month period is 91 days and the one-month period is 30 days.

Analysis
The bank can:

	%
Borrow for three months at 4.25%:	
Cost 4.25% x 91/360	-1.074306
Invest for one month at 4.12%	
Income 4.12% x 30/360	+0.343333
Sell a 1 v 3 FRA at 4.32%	
Income 4.32% x 61/360	+0.732000
Net surplus	+0.001027

The figures in this example are rather extreme. However, the opportunity exists here for the bank to make an immediate profit by borrowing for three months at euribor, lending for one month at euribor and selling a 1 v 3 FRA. This arbitrage opportunity occurs because the 1 v 3 FRA is mispriced, and the rate obtainable should be lower.

Speculation and FRAs

In theory, FRAs could be used to speculate on future movements in short-term interest rates. An organization speculating on an unexpected rise in interest rates could buy FRAs, and selling FRAs could be a method of speculating on unexpected falls in interest rates. The speculator would incur no transaction costs, and there would be no receipt or payment of cash until settlement date.

Local legislation might prohibit the use of FRAs for speculative purposes, for example in the UK, under its gaming laws. However, a situation might arise where an FRA that has been bought or sold to hedge an existing exposure on an underlying loan or investment is no longer required because the underlying loan or investment for some reason ceases to exist. The FRA will then become speculative.

Banks trading FRAs inevitably take on interest-rate exposures by arranging to buy and sell FRAs. However, they will hedge their positions, usually by taking offsetting positions in the interest-rate futures market by buying or selling interest-rate futures.

Arranging an FRA

FRAs are used primarily by banks and some large non-bank organizations.

An organization wishing to arrange an FRA is likely to approach one or more price-competitive banks in the FRA market. Alternatively it might use a money-market broker to obtain the most favorable rate available without initially having to disclose its identity.

An FRA is negotiated by telephone, and the details are then confirmed in writing. It is then issued as a formal contract that the customer signs. In the UK, a standard form of FRA agreement has been developed by the British Bankers' Association, whose terms in this agreement are known as FRABBA terms.

Canceling an FRA

An FRA is an over-the-counter agreement. Because it is not exchange-traded, it is not marketable.

An organization that has bought or sold an FRA subsequently might find that, prior to settlement date, it no longer needs or wants it, and decides to cancel. There are two ways of canceling an FRA:

- by negotiation with the bank that is the counterparty to the FRA, or
- with another bank.

Cancelation by reversal means transacting an FRA in the opposite direction, i.e. selling an FRA to cancel a purchased FRA, or buying an FRA to cancel a sold FRA. The new FRA will be for the same interest period as the original agreement, and the rate will be the current rate obtainable in the market.

Example
On 1 June, an organization bought a 3 v 6 FRA on £20 million. One month later, it finds that it has no requirement for the FRA, and decides to cancel it by reversal. There are two ways it might do this.

- It can approach the bank from which it bought the FRA. This bank will be asked to cancel the FRA by quoting a rate for a 2 v 5 FRA with the same settlement date as the original 3 v 6 FRA. A net payment to settle the two FRA transactions then can be established, based on the difference between the rates in the two FRA agreements. The cancelation payment probably will be made immediately, instead of waiting for the settlement date of the two agreements in two months' time.
- If the organization is not satisfied with the cancelation terms offered, it can approach another bank and sell a 2 v 5 FRA with the same settlement date and notional principal amount as the original 3 v 6 FRA. Both agreements will be settled on the same date in two months' time.

The effect of cancelation of an FRA is to fix the net payment or receipt that the organization must make. It removes the exposure to adverse interest-rate movements between the date of cancelation and the settlement date for the original FRA.

What are Futures?

Purpose and Characteristics of Futures

A futures contract is a type of forward contract or forward price agreement. There are two parties to a futures transaction, a buyer and a seller. The parties agree to buy/sell a quantity of an item for delivery and settlement at an agreed future date. The price is agreed when the contract is made.

Futures are for trading price risk. A futures contract fixes the price of the underlying item in advance of delivery/settlement date.

Characteristics of a futures contract that distinguish it from an over-the-counter forward contract or forward price agreement are as follows:

- Futures are exchange-traded. They are bought and sold on a futures exchange and are not traded over-the-counter.
- They are **standardized** contracts in the underlying item. With the exception of their settlement date, every futures contract for a particular underlying item and traded on a particular futures exchange, has exactly the same specifications as every other futures contract for that item. For example, all futures contracts in pork bellies traded on the Chicago Mercantile Exchange (CME) have exactly the same specifications, except for settlement date: in particular, every contract is for the same quantity of the underlying item and for a specified quality standard.
- The specifications for futures contracts, and their settlement/delivery dates, are specified by the futures exchange that trades them. The rules and procedures for trading in futures are

specified by the futures exchange.

The market for a futures contract has to be liquid. Contracts for a given settlement date should trade in significant quantities right up to settlement date itself. A liquid market is important because:

- it should be possible at all times to find a willing buyer or seller to act as counterparty in a futures transaction, and so
- prices in the market will always be fair.

Origins of the Futures Markets

The origins of futures date back to the 1860s and the Chicago grain markets. Grain prices were extremely volatile, with unpredictable supply and demand, and this price volatility created significant business risks. Grain farmers never could be sure what price they would get for their next grain crop, and buyers of grain never could be sure what price they would have to pay.

In 1848, a group of grain merchants set up the Chicago Board of Trade (CBOT) for the purpose of bringing greater price stability to the markets and reducing price uncertainty. Initially, the CBOT acted as a meeting point for negotiating forward contracts in grain: these were contracts between two parties for the delivery of a quantity of grain at a future date, at a price agreed in advance, in the contract.

By the 1860s, standardized contracts in grain were being traded. A standardized contract was for a fixed quantity of grain of a given quality specification. Futures therefore evolved out of over-the-counter forward contracts.

The Implications of Standardization

Standardization of forward price contracts had some important implications.

- Because every futures contract was for a given quantity and quality specification of an item, the key bargaining factor in buying and selling futures was price alone.
- Standardization made contracts easy to buy and sell. A large and liquid futures market therefore could develop, with forward prices readily available at any time up to delivery/settlement date for a contract.
- A large and liquid market in futures created opportunities for dealing in futures without having to take possession of the underlying item. Dealers could trade in grain futures without ever having either to take physical possession of any grain or deliver any grain. Trading in grain was separated from trading in the price risk of grain.
- The ability of a dealer in futures to specialize in price risk, without having to trade in the underlying item, encouraged speculation in prices by some dealers. Where prices of the underlying item are volatile, speculation can have a beneficial effect on the market, by providing greater price stability.

Settlement of Contracts

Futures contracts have differing specifications. Some contracts require the delivery of the underlying item at settlement/delivery date.

Other contracts are cash settled: these include all contracts where the underlying item is a notional item, such as a notional amount of principal (short-term interest-rate futures) or a notional quantity of equity stocks (stock index futures). Cash settlement involves a payment by one party to settle the contract and a corresponding receipt by the other party. One party in effect pays the other for the difference between the price fixed in the futures transaction and the reference price for the item at settlement. Cash settlement of futures is similar in concept to the payment of compensation on settlement of an FRA.

Closing a Position Before Delivery

Futures are traded for a specific settlement/delivery date. However, instead of waiting until settlement to conclude the transaction, someone holding a position in futures can close the position at any time up to settlement date. On closing the position, there will be an overall gain or loss on the futures transactions.

- Someone who has bought futures contracts is said to be long in the futures or to hold a long position. A long position can be closed by selling an equal number of the contracts for the same settlement date. For example, someone who has purchased 100 June sterling LIBOR futures can close the position by selling 100 June sterling LIBOR futures at any time before settlement date in June.
- Someone who has sold futures contracts is said to be short in the futures or to hold a short position. A short position can be closed by purchasing an equal number of the contracts for the same settlement date. For example, someone who has sold 200 September German government bond (Bund) futures can close the position by buying 200 September Bund futures at any time before settlement date in September.

The ability to establish either long or short positions, and to close positions at any time before delivery/settlement date, adds considerably to the flexibility of futures contracts as instruments for managing price risk or for price speculation, provided that the market in the futures contract is liquid, so that positions can be opened and closed readily at any time and at a fair price.

Trading in the Underlying Item and Trading Price Risk

Futures trading separates the trading in price risk from trading in the underlying item.

Suppose for example that a grain farmer is worried about the price he will get for his grain later in the year. He can arrange to sell grain futures, thereby fixing in advance the effective price he will get for his grain.

When the grain is available for delivery, the grain farmer can sell the grain direct to a grain dealer at the current market price. At the same time, he can close his futures position by purchasing grain futures, and will make an overall profit or loss on his futures transactions. The profit or loss will be the difference between the prices at which he sold and bought the futures contracts.

The actual price received for the grain, plus the profit or minus the loss on the futures transactions, will give him an effective price for the grain that will be the price, or close to the price, at which he sold the original futures.

Although this example uses a physical commodity as the underlying item, the same concept applies to using interest-rate futures.

Specifications of Futures Contracts

Futures contracts have certain specifications, established by the futures exchange. They include:

- the nature and quantity of the underlying item
- delivery/settlement date
- the method of delivery (physical delivery or cash settlement)
- how the reference price for the item is fixed, for the purpose of settlement
- the minimum price movement in the contract
- the value of each unit of price movement.

The Underlying Item

Futures are traded for a wide range of items.

Agricultural futures
These include futures in grain (wheat, maize, barley, etc.), soya (soyabeans, soyabean oil, soyabean meal) and meat and livestock (live cattle, lean hogs and pork bellies).

Energy futures
These include futures in crude oil, heating oil, gas oil, natural gas and unleaded gasoline.

Metals futures
There are futures in base metals (aluminium, aluminium alloy, lead, nickel, tin, zinc and copper) and precious metals (gold, platinum, palladium and silver).

Futures in softs
These include futures in cocoa, coffee, sugar, cotton and orange juice.

Other commodities
There are futures contracts in a variety of other commodities, such as lumber and pulp and paper.

Financial futures consist principally of stock index futures, currency futures and interest-rate futures.

Stock index futures
For stock index futures, the underlying item is a notional portfolio of shares that constitute a stockmarket index. Movements in the futures price reflect movements in the stockmarket index. Stock index futures are traded in most major stock market indices, such as Standard & Poor's 500, the FTSE 100, the CAC-40, the DAX and the Nikkei 225.

Currency futures
The world's leading exchange for trading currency futures is the Chicago Mercantile Exchange (International Monetary Market division). The underlying item is a quantity of one currency deliverable in exchange for another currency, and the futures price is an exchange rate. The major contracts are for the dollar against the euro, the Japanese yen, the Swiss franc and sterling.

Interest-rate futures

There are short-term interest-rate futures (STIRs) and bond futures. For short-term interest-rate futures, the underlying item is commonly a notional deposit for a given term, e.g. a three-month deposit of dollars. For bond futures, the underlying item is a quantity of notional bonds.

Standard Quantities

For each futures contract, there is a standard quantity of the underlying item, such as 100 tons of wheat, 1,000 barrels of crude oil, a notional portfolio of shares, a notional three-month deposit of $1 million or $100,000 (nominal value) of notional US Treasury bonds.

Someone wishing to trade a larger quantity of the underlying item must buy or sell an appropriate quantity of contracts. For example, if the underlying quantity is 100 tons of wheat, someone wishing to buy futures for 2,000 tons of wheat would have to buy 20 wheat futures contracts. Similarly, someone wishing to sell futures on $1 million of notional US Treasuries would have to sell 10 contracts.

There are also quality standards for the underlying item that are either specified or implied, so that futures contracts provide standardization of quality as well as quantity. Quality might relate, for example, to purity in the case of metals futures. For short-term interest-rate futures, the quality is implied because the underlying deposit will earn interest at a benchmark rate of interest, such as three-month sterling LIBOR. For bond futures, the quality is implied when the notional bonds are risk-free (notional government bonds).

Delivery Dates

A futures contract has:

- a last trading day and

- a delivery and settlement date.

The last trading day is the last day on which contracts for delivery/ settlement in that month can be traded. In the case of short-term interest-rate futures, for example, delivery day is a specified time on the business day before delivery day.

Delivery day and settlement day are when buyers and sellers must carry out the terms of their contract.

Most buyers and sellers of futures do not keep their positions open until delivery day; instead, they close their positions before delivery day. However, some positions are kept open, and these must be settled in accordance with the rules and procedures of the exchange.

Depending on the rules of the exchange for the particular contract, delivery and settlement might involve:

- actual delivery of the underlying item for the price originally agreed in the contract, or
- a cash settlement, without any exchange of the underlying item.

Short-term interest-rate futures are cash-settled, and in this respect are similar to FRAs.

Delivery Months

Each type of futures contract is traded for at least four delivery days each year, in March, June, September and December.

Contracts often are referred to by their delivery day, e.g. March eurodollar futures or December Bund futures.

In addition, contract might be traded for delivery in the near months.

Prices can be obtained and contracts can be traded for up to several years ahead, depending on the size and liquidity of the market for the particular contract. Most trading, however, is in near-dated contracts.

Futures Pricing

Each type of futures contract is priced in a particular way, reflecting the way in which the underlying item is priced in the markets. The price might be expressed, for example, in dollars per ton, cents per pound weight, as an exchange rate (currency futures), as a stockmarket index level (stock index futures), or as a bond price. The prices of short-term interest rates are quoted as 100 minus the annual rate of interest on the underlying deposit: for example, a price of 94.00 represents an interest rate of 6.00%.

There are several aspects of price.

- *Contract price.* This is the price at which the futures contract was agreed originally between buyer and seller. This is one of the prices that will determine the gain or loss on futures trading when the contracts are settled at delivery day, or when the position is closed.
- *Market price.* Futures are traded continually and prices at which contracts are made inevitably vary. Prices will rise or fall in response to market conditions and changing expectations about future price movements up to delivery day. The futures exchange will receive transaction data and reports transaction price data through its information distribution system. This ensures that traders are kept fully informed about current prices in the market.
- *Daily settlement price.* At the end of each trading day, the exchange authorities establish a closing price for a future. This is based on transaction prices in the short time before the end of the day's trading, and it becomes the exchange's daily settlement price for the contract. The daily settlement price is used to calculate the profit or loss on futures positions, and the change in the profit or loss since the previous day. This is a process known as marking to market. The daily settlement price can be used by traders to monitor their positions, and also is used to establish the amount of variation margin required to

cover a position. Variation margin is explained in a later chapter.

- *Exchange Delivery Settlement Price (EDSP).* On the last trading day for a contract, the exchange authorities decide the Exchange Delivery Settlement Price or EDSP. This, together with the contract price, is used to decide what payments are due on cash-settled contracts on delivery/settlement day. For example, if a trader buys June FTSE 100 stock index futures at 6,200 and the EDSP in June is 6,350 for example, the trader will have made a gain of 150 stock index points at settlement.

Price Changes: Ticks

When the market price of futures goes up, there is a gain for holders of long positions in the contract, i.e.buyers. A fall in the futures price provides a gain for holders of short positions (sellers).

Each contract has a unit of price, known as a **tick**. This is the minimum price movement in the contract. When prices go up or down, the price change can be stated in terms of the number of ticks the price has risen or fallen. For example, if the tick for a contract is 0.01, a fall in price of 0.05 would be a fall of five ticks. If the tick for a contract is 0.005, a fall in price of 0.05 would represent a fall of 10 ticks.

For each futures contract, a tick has a fixed value. This is the change in value in the underlying item for the future multiplied by the change in its price. For example, suppose the tick for an oil future is $0.01 (one cent) and the underlying item is 1,000 tons of oil. Each tick of price movement will represent a rise or fall of $10 (1,000 x $0.01) in the value of the contract.

Measuring price changes in ticks means that gains or losses in futures positions can be calculated easily and simply, in terms of a number of ticks and a value per tick. For example, suppose that the value of a tick is $10. If the value of a future goes up by 16 ticks for example, there will be a gain of $160 per contract for a holder of a long position in the contract and a corresponding loss of $160 for the holder of a short position. Someone with a long position of 50 contracts therefore would make a profit of $8,000 (16 ticks x $10 per tick x 50 contracts) on the position, given a price rise of 16 ticks.

Futures Exchanges

There are a large number of futures exchanges around the world. Each exchange specializes in one or more types of future. The specifications for a contract, underlying item, quantity, quality standards, delivery days, tick size, and so on, are decided by the authorities of the exchange where the contract is traded.

Futures traded by one exchange cannot be traded on another exchange. There are occasional exceptions to this rule, where two or more exchanges collaborate to trade the same contract.

The contracts traded by a futures exchange vary over time as unsuccessful contracts are scrapped and new contracts are introduced.

Futures exchanges that trade various financial futures include:

- The Chicago Board of Trade (CBOT)
- The Chicago Mercantile Exchange (CME). Financial futures are traded in the International Monetary Market (IMM) division of the exchange
- Eurex that is a futures exchange created by the merger of the Deutsche Terminbörse (based in Frankfurt) and the Swiss Soffex exchange
- The London International Financial Futures Exchange (LIFFE)
- The Marché à Terme Internationale de France (Matif) in Paris
- The Singapore Money Exchange (SIMEX) that has a link with the CME.

Exchanges might compete to attract business. LIFFE, for example, has competed with Eurex and the Matif. LIFFE has succeeded in attracting most of the trading in short-term interest rates for the euro, whereas Eurex was successful in attracting the trading in German government-bond futures.

Summary

Financial futures are standardized exchange-traded instruments that are used for trading in price risk for an underlying item. They can be used to hedge an exposure to the risk of unfavorable price movements in the item in the period up to delivery day for the contract. They can be used to speculate on price movements also.

Futures are bought and sold at an agreed (contract) price, for a set delivery day. The price of the future reflects the price of the underlying item that can be an agricultural commodity, another type of commodity, a quantity of metal, a notional stockmarket portfolio, a quantity of currency, a quantity of notional bonds or a notional short-term deposit.

Each futures contract is for a standard quantity of the underlying item. To trade in larger amounts, a quantity of contracts must be traded.

Futures contracts are traded on a futures exchange. Each exchange has a different range of contracts for trading. The standard contract specifications are decided by the exchange authorities.

Someone buying futures for a given delivery date, without previously having sold futures, is said to hold a long position. Someone selling futures without previously having bought any is said to hold a short position. Price rises benefit holders of long positions and give rise to a loss for holders of short positions. Price falls create losses on long positions and gains on short positions.

Positions in a contract can be kept open until delivery day. On delivery day, positions are settled, either by physical delivery of the underlying item at the contract price, or by means of cash settlement. The amount of the cash settlement is based on the difference between the contract price and the Exchange Delivery Settlement Price.

Futures positions normally are closed before delivery day. A long position is closed by selling an equal number of contracts for the same delivery day. A short position is closed by purchasing an equal number of contracts. The overall gain or loss on closing a position is the difference between the original purchase or sale price and the subsequent sale or purchase price on closing the position.

Gains or losses on futures positions are monitored and measured by movements in the price of the future. Each contract has a minimum price movement, or tick. Each tick has a standard value. The gain or loss on a futures position therefore can be measured in terms of number of ticks multiplied by value per tick multiplied by number of futures contracts.

Short-Term Interest-Rate Futures (STIRs)

Interest-rate futures are either short-term interest-rate futures or bond futures. This chapter focuses on short-term interest-rate futures, or STIRs. Most of these have similar characteristics, with respect to:

- the underlying item
- a reference interest rate
- pricing
- delivery/settlement.

The Underlying Item for a STIR

The underlying item for any short-term interest-rate future must be an item whose price or value is a measure of money-market interest rates. For most STIR futures, the underlying item is a notional short-term deposit of a given period, typically of three months, and for a standard principal amount.

Alternatively, the underlying item might be a quantity of notional Treasury bills.

Examples are:

Contract	Exchange	Underlying item
Three-month eurodollar	CME	Notional three-month deposit of $1 million
13-week US Treasury bill	CME	$1 million (nominal value) of notional 13-week US Treasury bills
Three-month euribor	LIFFE	Notional three-month deposit of €1 million, paying interest at the EBF euribor rate
Three-month euro Libor	LIFFE	Notional three-month deposit of €1 million, paying interest at the BBA LIBOR rate
Three-month sterling (short sterling)	LIFFE	Notional three-month deposit of £500,000, paying interest at the BBA LIBOR rate
Three-month euro Swiss franc	LIFFE	Notional three-month deposit of SFr1 million
Three-month euroyen	LIFFE	Notional three-month deposit of ¥100 million

The buyer of a eurodollar future, for example, is buying a notional three-month deposit of $1 million starting on delivery day for the contract. The price at which the future is purchased reflects the interest rate that will be receivable on the deposit.

Similarly, the seller of a three-month euribor future is providing a notional three-month deposit of €1 million starting on delivery day for the contract. The price at which the future is sold reflects the interest rate payable.

- Buying a short-term interest-rate future, where the underlying item is a notional deposit, fixes a short-term interest rate receivable at a future time.
- Selling a short-term interest-rate future, where the underlying item is a notional deposit, fixes an interest rate payable at a future time.

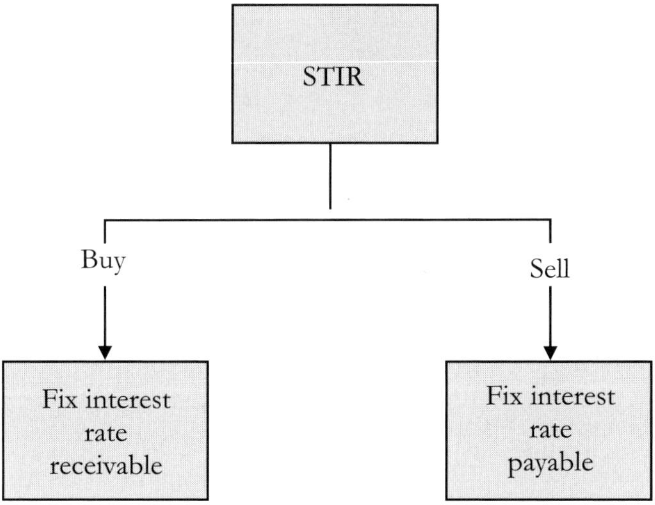

The Interest Rate

A short-term interest rate is priced on the basis of a money-market interest rate that is specified exactly in the contract.

The following examples are illustrative:

Contract	Exchange Delivery Settlement Price obtained by reference to
Three-month eurodollar	The British Bankers' Association London Offered Rate (BBA LIBOR) for three-month eurodollar deposits, as at 11.00 a.m. London time on the last trading day for the contract, rounded to the nearest 0.005% (0.0025% amounts are rounded down)
Three-month euribor	The European Bankers' Federation Euribor Offered Rate (EBF Euribor) for three-month deposits of euros, as at 11.00 a.m. Brussels time on the last trading day for the contract, rounded to the nearest 0.005% (0.0025%

	amounts are rounded down; for example 4.3675% would be rounded down to 4.365%)
Three-month euro Libor	The British Bankers' Association London Offered Rate (BBA LIBOR) for three-month euro deposits, as at 11.00 a.m. London time on the last trading day for the contract, rounded to the nearest 0.005% (0.0025% amounts are rounded down)
Short sterling	The British Bankers' Association London Offered Rate (BBA LIBOR) for three-month sterling deposits, as at 11.00 a.m. London time on the last trading day for the contract, rounded to the nearest 0.005% (0.0025% amounts are rounded down)
Three-month euro Swiss	The British Bankers' Association London Offered Rate (BBA LIBOR) for three-month Swiss franc deposits, as at 11.00 a.m. London time on the last trading day for the contract, rounded to the nearest 0.005% (0.0025% amounts are rounded down)
Three-month euroyen (LIBOR)	The British Bankers' Association London Offered Rate (BBA LIBOR) for three-month yen deposits, as at 11.00 a.m. London time on the last trading day for the contract.

Of the two benchmark interest rates for the euro, the euribor rate is more commonly used than the euro Libor rate. LIFFE trades futures in both, but the euribor contracts are more heavily traded.

Pricing Short-Term Interest-Rate Futures

Short-term interest-rate futures are priced at 100 minus the interest rate per annum on the notional deposit.

For example, a price of 94.00 represents an interest rate of 6.00% per annum, and a price of 94.90 represents an interest rate of 5.10%.

- Higher STIR prices represent lower interest rates.
- Lower STIR prices represent higher interest rates.

Example
Short-term eurodollar interest rates are as follows for the next four delivery dates, as at May:

Delivery month	Price
June	93.13
September	92.78
December	92.47
March	92.16

The interest rates indicated by these prices are 6.87% for June (100 – 93.13), 7.22% for September, 7.53% for December and 7.84% for March.

A buyer of a September eurodollar future at 92.78 would be fixing an interest rate receivable of 7.22% on a three-month dollar deposit of $1 million from delivery day in September.

Ticks for STIRs

The tick size for a short-term interest-rate contract is a price movement of either 0.005 or 0.01, depending on the specifications for the particular contract.

Contract	Tick size	Value of one tick
Three-month eurodollar	0.01	$25
13-week US Treasury bill	0.005	$12.50
Three-month euribor	0.005	€12.5
Three-month euro Libor	0.005	€12.5
Short sterling	0.01	£12.50
Three-month euro Swiss franc	0.01	SFr25
Three-month euroyen	0.005	¥1,250

The value of a tick is derived as follows:

- For the euribor contract: €1,000,000 x 3/12 x 0.005% = €12.50.
- For the short sterling contract:
  £500,000 x 3/12 x 0.01% = £12.50.
- For the eurodollar contract: $1,000,000 x 3/12 x 0.01% = $25.

Price Changes

Prices of short-term interest-rate futures fluctuate in response to changing money-market conditions and changing expectations of future interest rates in the period up to delivery day for the contract. This means, for example, that if delivery day is two months from now, the price of a short-term interest-rate future should be comparable with the current price of a 2 v 5 FRA.

If market expectations change, and interest rates are expected to be higher than previously expected by delivery day, the price of a future will fall.

Similarly, if expectations change and rates are expected to be lower than previously expected by delivery day, there will be a rise in the price of the future.

Futures Price Changes in Response to Interest-Rate Changes

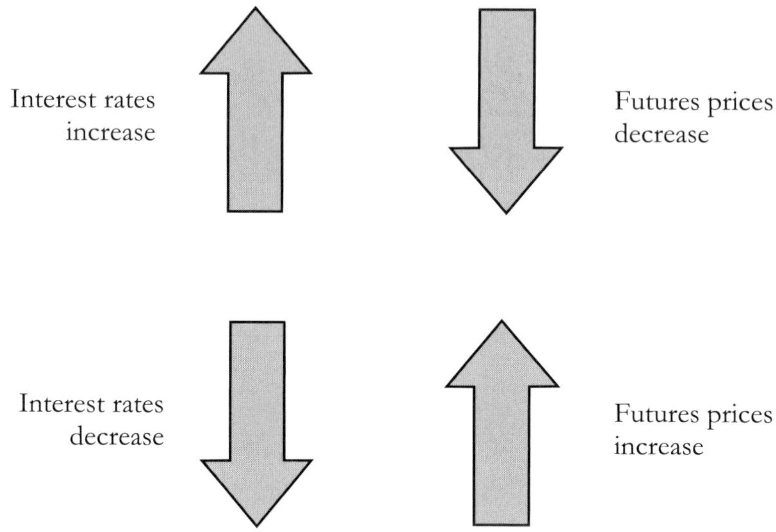

Short-term interest rates are priced at 100 minus the interest rate so that the futures prices will move in the opposite direction to changes in expected interest rates. There are two reasons for this.

- The movement in prices in the opposite direction to interest-rate changes is consistent with bond futures, i.e. long-term interest-rate futures.
- It means that a buyer of futures will benefit from a subsequent rise in prices and a seller will benefit from any subsequent fall in interest rates. It is logical that a buyer should benefit from a rise in prices, and that a seller should benefit from a drop in prices.

Who Benefits from Price Changes?

Someone who is long in short-term interest rate futures, i.e. a buyer, benefits from a fall in expected interest rates and a higher futures price.

Suppose for example that an organization establishes a long position in short sterling futures by purchasing 100 December contracts at 93.00. The organization is acquiring the right to receive an interest rate of

7.00% on notional sterling deposits from delivery day in December. Suppose now that expectations of interest rates on sterling change downwards, so that the December future rises in price to 93.50. The market is now expecting three-month interest rates of 6.50% in December, but the organization has futures that fixed a rate receivable of 7.00%. The gain on the organization's long position is 0.50%, because it has contracted to receive 0.50% more than the current market interest rate. A gain of 0.50, that is 50 ticks on the short sterling contract, has a value of:

100 contracts x 50 ticks per contract x £12.50 per tick = £62,500.

Someone who is short in short-term interest-rate futures, i.e. the seller, benefits from a rise in expected interest rates and a lower futures price.

Suppose for example that an organization establishes a short position in euribor futures by purchasing 200 September contracts at 95.00. The organization is acquiring the right to pay an interest rate of 5.00% on notional euro deposits from delivery day in September. Suppose that expectations of sterling interest rates change upwards, so that the September future falls in price to 94.75. The market is now expecting three-month interest rates of 5.25 % in September, but the organization has futures that fixed a rate payable of just 5.00%. The gain on the organization's short position is 0.25, that is 50 ticks for the euribor contract. This has a value of:

200 contracts x 50 ticks x €12.50 per tick = €125,000.

Delivery Dates for Short-Term Interest-Rate Futures

The delivery dates for short-term interest-rate futures are specified by the exchange. Examples are:

Contract	Delivery months	Delivery day	Last trading day
Eurodollar	March, June, September, December. Also four serial months and the spot month.	First business day after the last trading day	10.00, two business days prior to the third Wednesday of the delivery month
Euribor	March, June, September, December. Also two serial months, such that 22 delivery months are available for trading, with the next three delivery months being consecutive calendar months	First business day after the last trading day	10.00, two business days prior to the third Wednesday of the delivery month
Euro Libor	March, June, September, December. Also two serial months, such that 18 delivery months are available for trading, with the next three delivery months being consecutive calendar months	First business day after the last trading day	11.00, two business days prior to the third Wednesday of the delivery month

Contract	Delivery months	Delivery day	Last trading day
Short sterling	March, June, September, December. Also two serial months, such that 22 delivery months are available for trading, with the next three delivery months being consecutive calendar months	First business day after the last trading day	10.00, two business days prior to the third Wednesday of the delivery month
Euro Swiss franc	March, June, September, December. Also two serial months, such that 18 delivery months are available for trading, with the next three delivery months being consecutive calendar months	First business day after the last trading day	10.00, two business days prior to the third Wednesday of the delivery month

Marking to Market

Open positions in futures are marked to market daily. The exchange determines a daily settlement rate from prices in the closing range at the end of the day. The gains or losses on the day are used to assess margins payable. The payment of initial and variation margins is explained in another chapter.

Example

An organization has a long position in March eurodollar futures of 100 contracts. The contracts were bought at 94.00. The settlement price for the previous day was 94.76, and today's settlement price is 94.70.

Yesterday, the cumulative gain on the position was 0.76 ticks per contract:

100 contracts x 76 ticks x \$25 = \$190,000.

Because of the fall of 0.06 ticks today, the value of the position has fallen by:

100 contracts x 6 ticks x \$25 = \$15,000.

Closing a Position

An open position can be closed at any time before the last trading day by executing an offsetting transaction. On closing a position, an overall profit or loss on the futures transactions can be established.

Example
An organization sold 40 June euribor contracts at 95.80. Some weeks later, it closed its position by buying 40 June euribor contracts at 95.55.

The organization has made a profit on its futures transactions:

Sale price	95.80
Purchase price	95.55
Profit per contract	0.25

The profit per contract is 0.25, 50 ticks, and at a value of €12.50 per tick for 40 contracts, the overall profit is €(50 x 12.50 x 40) = €25,000.

Delivery/Settlement

Most futures positions are closed before delivery day. However, positions that remain open until settlement are cash-settled. The contract price is compared with an Exchange Delivery Settlement Price (EDSP), to establish the overall profit or loss.

Example

An organization purchased 20 December euro Swiss franc contracts at 95.90. It kept this position open to delivery, and the Exchange Delivery Settlement Price was 95.10.

The organization has made a loss on its futures transactions:

Purchase price	95.90
Settlement price	95.10
Loss per contract	0.80

The loss is 80 ticks per contract, and for 20 contracts, the total loss on the futures transactions is SFr(80 x 25 x 20) = SFr40,000.

Summary

This chapter has explained the *features* of short-term interest-rate futures.

Using interest-rate futures to hedge interest-rate risk, is the subject of a separate chapter.

6

Bond Futures

The Underlying Item

A bond future is a long-term interest-rate future for which the underlying item is a quantity of notional bonds, typically a quantity of notional government bonds.

The notional bonds have:

- a nominal value
- a fixed coupon (rate of interest)
- a remaining term to maturity of no less than and no more than a specified length of time.

The underlying item therefore is a quantity of fixed coupon bonds of a particular type, e.g. US Treasury bonds, and with a given maturity.

The reasons for having notional bonds rather than an actual issue of bonds are:

- standardization, and
- practicality.

Notional bonds are of a standard specification, and represent the bond market as a whole for bonds of a particular type and maturity range. For example, the long gilt future represents UK government bonds (gilts) generally with a maturity of 8.5 to 10.5 years.

If an actual bond issue were the underlying item, it would have to be replaced whenever its remaining term to maturity became less than the minimum maturity for which the futures are intended to be representative. Notional bonds retain the same time to maturity, unaffected by the passing of time.

Bond Futures and Hedging Exposure to Interest-Rate Risk

The prices of bonds of a similar type and maturity respond in broadly the same way in response to a change in market interest rates. Bond futures therefore can be used to hedge against the risk of adverse movements in bond prices, i.e. adverse movements in bond yields, for bonds of a given maturity range.

- The buyer of a bond future undertakes to buy a quantity of notional bonds, at a future delivery date, at an agreed price.
- The seller of a bond future undertakes to sell a quantity of notional bonds, at a future delivery date, at that price.

The price agreed in the futures contract effectively locks in a bond yield by fixing the price of the bonds, for bonds of that given maturity.

Contract Specifications

Bond futures are traded on a number of futures exchanges around the world. Specifications are shown here for some of the more heavily traded futures.

Contract	**Exchange**	**Nominal value of bonds/ Trading unit**	**Coupon**	**Maturity range**
US Treasury bond	CBOT	$100,000	6%	15 years +
Euro Bund (German govt bond)	Eurex	€100,000	6%	8.5-10.5 years
5-year eurobond	Matif	€100,000	3.5%	3.5 -5.5 years
Long gilt	LIFFE	£100,000	7%	8.75-13 years
Spanish govt bond	MEFF	€100,000	6.5%	30-year bond

Delivery Months

All contracts are for delivery in the months of March, June, September and December.

The exchange undertakes to make trading in contracts available for a minimum number of consecutive delivery months. For example, suppose the exchange undertakes to make trading available in a particular contract for the next three delivery months. In July of Year 1, there would be trading in contracts for delivery in September and December in Year 1 and March of Year 2. In practise, the heaviest trading is in contracts for the nearest delivery month.

Price Quotations for Bond Futures and Ticks

Bond futures prices are quoted in a similar way to the prices of the bonds.

Most bonds and futures are priced to two decimal places, with a par value of 100.00: for example, 103.41 and 96.72.

US Treasury bond futures are priced differently. They have a par value of 100, but units are priced in 32nds rather than hundredths. For example, with T bond futures:

- A price of 101 – 08 means 101 8/32
- A price of 87 – 16 means 87 16/32

Tick sizes and tick values are:

Contract	Exchange	Tick size	Tick value
US Treasury bond	CBOT	1/32	$31.25
Euro Bund	Eurex	0.01	€10
5-year Eurobond	Matif	0.01	€10
Long and 5-year gilt	LIFFE	0.01	£10
Spanish govt bond	MEFF	0.01	€10

The value of a tick is calculated simply as the tick size multiplied by the nominal value of the underlying bonds. A tick size of 0.01 is 0.01 of a point, i.e. 0.01 of one hundredth that is 0.0001. Therefore the value of a tick for the Euro Bund future for example, is €100,000 x 0.0001 = €10. Similarly, the value of a tick for the US T-bond future is $100,000 x 0.01 x 1/32 = $31.25.

Bond Prices, Futures Prices and Changes in Interest Rates

The price of a bond reflects long-term interest yields. Prices paid by bond investors reflect the interest receivable on the bonds to maturity, the capital repayment at redemption, and the yield to redemption required by bondholders.

- If interest rates go up, so that investors require a higher yield on their bonds, prices of bonds in the market will fall.
- A fall in bond yields will push up the market prices of bonds.

The same applies to the prices of bond futures. An expected increase in bond yields in the period to delivery will push bond futures prices down. An anticipated fall in bond yields will push bond futures prices up.

Price Limits on Futures

Some exchanges apply daily price limits to movements in the price of a future. For example:

- The CBOT's Treasury bond future has a daily price limit of three points above or below the previous day's settlement price, although this limit is lifted on the second business day preceding the beginning of the delivery month.
- The Matif applies a daily price limit of plus or minus 80 basis points (0.80 in price) to the five-year eurobond future.

Marking-to-Market

Positions in bond futures are marked-to-market daily, and gains or losses are recorded on the position holder's account with the clearing house of the exchange (for the accounts of clearing members) and of the clearing members (for the accounts of their clients).

Example
An organization bought 20 September US Treasury bond futures at 94 – 05. The price at the previous day's settlement was 92 – 27. The exchange's daily settlement price today is 92 – 30.

Analysis
Up to the previous day, there is a cumulative loss on the position,

Purchase price	94 – 05
Yesterday's settlement price	92 – 27
Cumulative loss per contract (ticks)	1 - 10

The price has fallen from 94 5/32 to 92 27/32. This is a fall of one whole point (32/32) and a further 10/32, i.e. a fall of 42/32 or 42 ticks.

The value per tick is $31.25; therefore the overall cumulative loss on the position to yesterday was:

20 contracts x 42 ticks x $31.25 per tick = $26,250.

Marking-to-market today shows a rise in the price of three ticks, from 92 – 27 to 92 – 30. The gain on the position today therefore is:

20 contracts x 3 ticks x $31.25 per tick = $1,875.

This reduces the cumulative loss on the position to $24,375.

Closing Bond Positions Before Delivery

Positions in bond futures can be closed before delivery by means of an offsetting transaction. This is the same as for closing a position in any other type of future.

For example, a long position in 15 June futures can be closed by selling 15 June futures before delivery in June.

Example
An organization sold 30 March Euro Bund futures at 105.26. It closed its position by purchasing 30 March Euro Bund futures at 104.43.

Analysis
There has been a gain on the position.

Sale price	105.26
Buying price to close position	104.43
Gain per contract (ticks)	0.83

The total gain has been:

30 contracts x 83 ticks per contract x €10 per tick = €24,900.

Delivery

For futures positions that remain open to delivery, the rules about delivery and settlement are fairly complex.

A system of physical delivery operates for most bond futures contracts. A quantity of actual bonds is delivered by the seller to a buyer, and the buyer must pay for them at a price decided by the exchange, together with any accrued interest on the actual bonds.

The last trading day and the final delivery day for various bond futures contracts are as follows:

	Last trading day	Delivery day
US Treasury bond (CBOT)	12.00 on seventh business day preceding the last day of the delivery month	Last business day of the delivery month
Euro Bund (Eurex)	12.30 CET, second business day prior to delivery day	Tenth calendar day of the delivery month (or the next business day, if the tenth is not a business day)
Long gilt (LIFFE)	11.00, two business days prior to the last business day of the delivery month	Any business day in the delivery month, at the seller's choice

For gilt futures, the seller must give notice of an intention to settle the contract by physical delivery. The first notice day is two business days prior to the first day of the delivery month: the last notice day is the first business day after the last trading day.

An exception to the general rule that bond futures can be settled by physical delivery is the Japanese government bond future traded on LIFFE. The last trading day for this contract is 16.00 hrs on the London business day prior to the last trading day for the similar Japanese government bond futures traded on the Tokyo Stock Exchange. However, all open positions in the future on LIFFE at the close of a business day will be closed out automatically the next business day, at the subsequent opening price for the same future on the Tokyo Stock Exchange. The position is cash-settled.

The underlying item for a bond future is a quantity of notional bonds, but settlement by physical delivery requires the delivery of actual bonds by seller to a buyer The futures exchange provides a list of actual bonds that are acceptable. However, certain adjustments have to be made to ensure that, on physical delivery, the actual bonds are of an equivalent value to the notional bonds. The process of physical delivery is described in more detail in a later chapter.

7

Market Trading, Clearing and Settlement

Who Can Trade?

At one time, futures exchanges were member-owned mutual organizations, and firms or individuals wishing to trade on an exchange had to buy their way into membership. Most futures exchanges have now either demutualized or are in the process of doing so and establishing themselves as profit-making companies.

Firms trading on an exchange as members might act as brokers on behalf of clients, as well as on their own account. Other traders, known perhaps as locals, trade on their own account only, and do not act for clients. Organizations or individuals without exchange membership, but wishing to make transactions in futures, must go through a broker who will charge a commission for the service.

Electronic Trading and Open Outcry
Trading on a futures exchange is done either by open outcry or electronically.

Open outcry was the traditional trading system for futures, each futures contract had its own trading area or pit on the floor of the exchange. Within each pit, there was dealing in the contract, for each available delivery month.

Traders, wearing brightly coloured jackets to identify their firm (clearing member) or local status, shouted out their prices or communicated by hand signals. These indicated prices, whether the floor trader wanted to buy or sell, and the number of contracts. During busy trading sessions, pits got crowded with traders, who were likely to push and jostle for attention, as well as shout and signal. At one time, the Chicago Mercantile Exchange in its publicity material described open outcry as 'a type of free-form auction that combines elements of primal scream, aerobic dancing and the Battle of Hastings'.

Many futures exchanges, including Eurex, LIFFE and the Matif, now use electronic trading systems only, rather than open outcry. Following the commercial success of the electronic system of the Deutsche Terminbörse in Frankfurt, now part of the Eurex exchange, other exchanges switched from open outcry to electronic trading.

Open outcry has been retained by the Chicago Board of Trade and the Chicago Mercantile Exchange, although both have developed a complementary electronic trading system.

- CBOT has a link with Eurex and uses a common platform, referred to as alliance/cbot/eurex or a/c/e.
- CME is part of an alliance of exchanges using a trading system called Globex.

Order Process

Orders to buy or sell futures go through a member of the exchange. Non-members must go through a broker who is a member of the exchange.

Orders might be given by telephone or data link. The broker executes the order, if possible, on behalf of the client. If an electronic order trading system is used, the order is input to the system. Where open outcry is used, the broker will send the order to the floor of the exchange to be executed on its behalf by a floor trader.

Types of order include:

- Buy at the best price obtainable. This order always should be executed.
- Sell at the best price obtainable. This order also always should be executed.
- Market-if-touched. This is an order to buy only if the available price falls to, or touches, a specified level or below, or an order to sell only if the available price reaches a specified level or higher. This order might not be executed, depending on whether or not prices touch the level specified.
- Stop order. This is an order to buy if the available price rises to a certain level, or an order to sell if the available price falls to a certain level. This order might not be executed, depending on whether the specified price level is reached.

Orders from a client therefore must specify:

- the contract and delivery month
- the type of order, including whether to buy or sell
- the number of contracts
- where appropriate, a price, e.g. for a market-if-touched order or a stop order.

An order, once executed, is confirmed to the client. The exchange authorities feed the price details into its price-reporting system, and the transaction is registered.

Pricing Information

Ready access to current price information is essential for the efficient operation of the market. Prices at which transactions have been made are disseminated by the exchange and through information vendors such as Reuters and Bloomberg.

Price information can be presented in different ways.

Screen-based information might be presented as follows:

11.25		LIFFE	S-STG	FUTURES						
MTH	LAST	LT - 1	LT - 2	LT - 3	HIGH	LOW	VOLUM	OPEN	PR.SET	TIME
SEP	9375	9374	9375	9374	9377	9372	25,640	9373	9371	1125
DEC	9382	9383	9383	9381	9387	9379	6,582	9386	9384	1125
MAR	9389	9389	9388	9389	9392	9385	2,866	9391	9389	1123
JUN	9394	9392	9394	9395	9396	9391	1,239	9393	9393	1116
SEP	9399	9397	9398	9397	9404	9397	874	9402	9400	1120
DEC	9399	9399	9398	9397	9405	9397	534	9405	9403	1121
MAR	9405	9404	9403	9404	9406	9401	426	9406	9404	1015
JUN	9412	9410	9409	9410	9415	9408	450	9410	9407	1001
SEP	9416	9415	9417	9417	9419	9414	212	9415	9412	0956

In this table, showing prices for short sterling futures for future delivery months:

- the current time (GMT) is 11.25.
- The price of the most recent transaction is shown in the column headed LAST, and the prices of the three transactions before that in the LT – 1, LT – 2 and LT – 3 columns.
- The HIGH and LOW columns show the highest and lowest prices reached in the day's trading.
- VOLUM is the number of transactions.
- OPEN is the price at the opening of the day's trading session.
- PR.SET is the settlement price at the close of the previous day. This need not be the same as the opening price for the current day.
- Prices are shown without the decimal point, so that 9383, for example, means 93.83.

A financial newspaper might summarize the previous day's trading in a form as follows:

Three month Euribor futures (LIFFE): €1 million. 100 – rate

	Open	Sett Price	Change	High	Low	Est vol	Open int
Sep	95.580	95.605	+0.010	95.635	95.570	51970	317508
Dec	95.300	95.340	+0.025	95.370	95.295	58701	322531
Mar	95.030	95.070	+0.025	95.105	95.020	34103	192742
Jun	94.930	94.965	+0.025	95.000	94.920	20070	154292
Sep	94.800	94.840	+0.025	94.880	94.790	13455	100916
Dec	94.705	94.740	+0.025	94.780	94.700	7060	80937

Meanings:

- Open — Price at the start of trading on the day reported
- Sett Price — The exchange's daily settlement price for the day reported
- Change — The change between the day's settlement price and the previous day's settlement price
- High/low — Highest and lowest prices reached during the day
- Est vol — Estimated volume of transactions
- Open int — Number of contracts for which positions are still open.

Daily Price Limits

Some futures contracts on some exchanges are not permitted to move in price, up or down, by more than a specified limit in any single day. In other words, there is a maximum price fluctuation.

The purpose of a maximum price fluctuation is to ensure stability in the trading system. Large and sudden price changes could give rise to panic buying or selling, or destabilizing program trades.

Clearing and the Role of the Clearing House

Each futures exchange has a clearing house to administer the clearing and settlement of transactions.

The clearing house of a futures exchange performs a number of key functions:

- It matches purchases and sales transactions from the two sides to a transaction and registers the transactions.
- It becomes the counterparty to each side of the transaction. It becomes the seller for the clearing member that carried out the purchase, and it becomes the buyer for the clearing member that carried out the sale. The buyer and the seller deal with the clearing house, not with each other. The process of substituting the clearing house as buyer and seller to each side of the transaction is known as novation.
- The clearing house becomes responsible for ensuring that each party to a transaction on the exchange fulfills its obligations.
- To protect its financial position, the clearing house takes margin payments or performance-bond payments from all buyers and sellers of futures. Margin protects the clearing house against counterparty risk, i.e. the risk that a clearing member will fail to carry out its obligations and will incur losses on its positions that it cannot cover.
- It calculates the overall gain or loss on members' positions.
- It arranges for delivery/settlement of contracts.

The clearing house of the exchange will enter a transaction only with a clearing member of the exchange. Some members of a futures exchange are not clearing members. Non-clearing members must arrange for a clearing member to act on their behalf in dealing with the clearing house.

The Exchange (Clearing House) as Counterparty

In a normal business sale transaction, the buyer and the seller have a contractual obligation to each other. For futures trading, this is not the case. When a buyer and seller make a transaction, and the exchange is notified, the clearing house of the exchange steps between the buyer and seller and becomes:

- the buyer to the seller and
- the seller to the buyer.

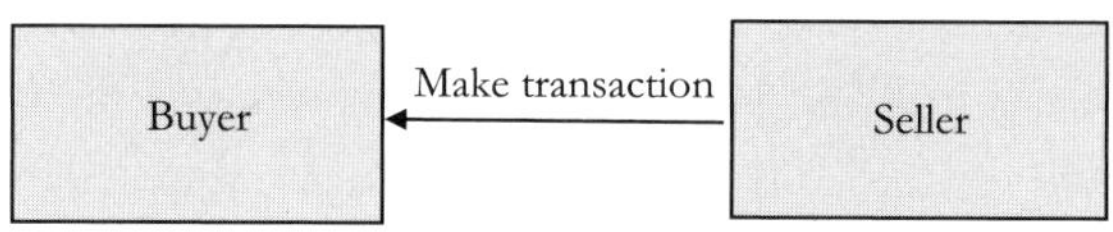

In dealing with the clearing house, the buyer and seller are represented by a clearing member of the exchange.

The contractual obligations are between:

- the buyer, i.e. the clearing member acting for the buyer, and the clearing house and
- the seller, i.e. the clearing member acting for the seller, and the clearing house.

Clearing members of an exchange:

- deal with each other, perhaps by electronic trading system, to buy and sell, but
- deal with the clearing house for administrative issues, such as confirmation of trades, payment of margin and eventual delivery/settlement of positions.

Why Should the Exchange Act as Counterparty?

A futures exchange must protect its reputation for financial integrity; otherwise financial institutions will not use it for transactions. The exchange therefore has to be a low-risk environment. By becoming the counterparty to every buyer and seller, the credit risk/counterparty risk for anyone dealing on the exchange is just the risk that the exchange itself will default on its contractual obligations. The exchange protects itself from counterparty credit risk by taking margin payments from the other party.

Any clearing member wishing to deal on the exchange can make transactions with any other clearing member without having to consider the credit risk of the other party. This low-risk trading environment for clearing members has a beneficial knock-on effect for the clients of clearing members.

Because the clearing house is the other party to every transaction, clearing and settlement processes are simplified and more efficient. For example, suppose that an organization has a long position in futures of 20 contracts, it can close its position by making an offsetting selling transaction. Because the original purchase and the closing sale are contracts with the same counterparty (the clearing house) it is a relatively simple process to establish the gain or loss on the organization's overall transactions.

Margin (Performance Bond)

The futures exchange removes counterparty credit risk from buyers and sellers, but takes on the risk itself. The exchange (clearing house) has to protect itself against the risk of default by any clearing member, i.e. the risk of running up a large loss on a position and then being unable to provide money to cover the loss.

The exchange (clearing house) protects itself by taking cash deposits to cover possible future losses on positions and actual losses incurred on positions. The cash deposits are known as margin payments or performance bonds. Margin payments are made into a clearing member's margin account with the clearing house.

- When a clearing member opens a position, an initial cash deposit becomes payable to the clearing house. This is known as an initial margin or initial performance bond.
- The initial margin has to be sufficiently large to cover the foreseeable losses on a position in a day's trading.
- The clearing house keeps an individual account of the margin payments of each clearing member.
- The clearing member's daily gains or losses on positions are recorded in the account.
- If, because of losses on positions, the clearing member's account falls below a minimum required safety level, the clearing house makes a margin call and the clearing member will be required to make a further immediate payment to cover the losses already incurred. These additional margin payments are known as variation margin.
- An exchange might not call for additional margin as soon as losses of any size are made. Instead, it might wait until the balance on the clearing member's account falls below a minimum acceptable level, a maintenance margin level. If losses accumulate, and the balance on the account falls below this level, a further margin call will be made.
- If profits are earned on a position, the clearing member can withdraw the surplus from its margin account.

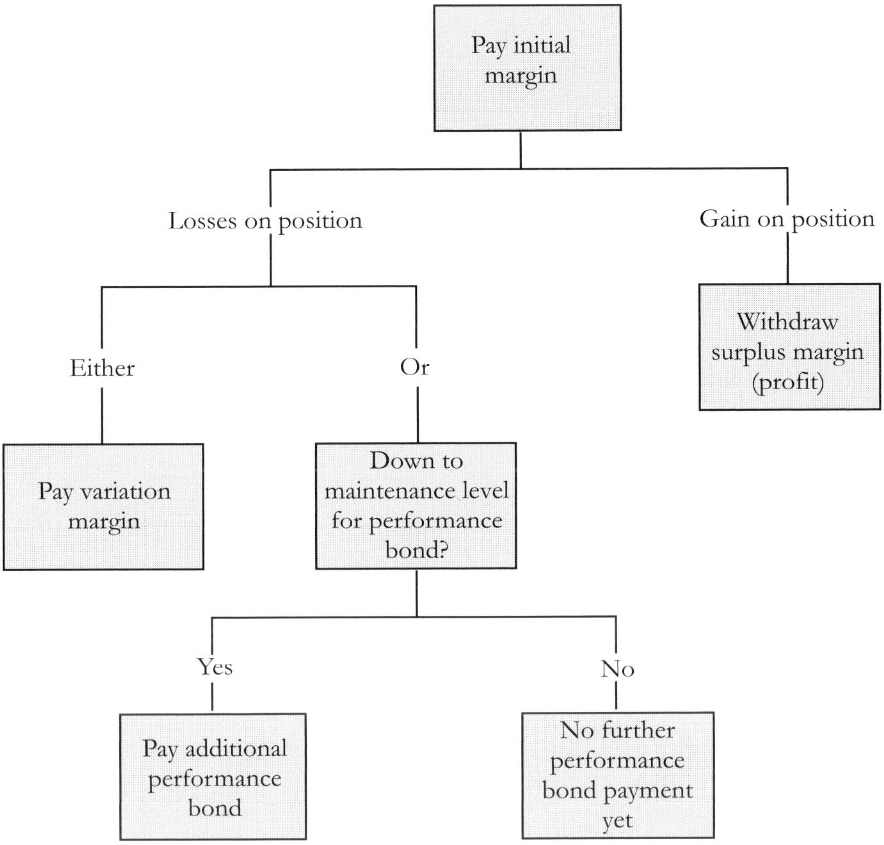

How Large Are Margin Payments?

The initial margin should be sufficient to cover any foreseeable daily loss on a futures position. The size of margin deposit required should reflect the potential adverse movements in the price of the future in any day. Variation margin payments should be sufficient to restore the margin in the clearing member's account to an amount sufficient to provide for the potential losses on a further day's trading. Where a position is continually loss-making, variation margin calls will be made regularly.

In principle, each contract bought or sold to create an open position should require a payment of margin to provide cover against possible losses on the position. In practise, more sophisticated risk analysis models are applied, and the amount of margin a clearing member is required to provide to the clearing house, and the margin some clients are required to provide to their broker, will be determined by the model.

The margining system used by the Chicago Mercantile Exchange or its clearing members is called SPAN (**S**tandard **P**ortfolio **An**alysis). This sets minimum margin requirements for its clearing members' accounts on the basis of the risk in the members' positions taken as a whole. The SPAN model assesses what a clearing members' entire portfolio might reasonably lose in one day, and a margin is then set for the entire portfolio to provide against the risk of this one-day loss. LIFFE uses a similar system, derived from the CME's SPAN system, known as London SPAN.

Just as clearing members of the exchange are required to provide margin to the clearing house, clients of clearing members/brokers are required to provide margin to the clearing member/broker. Brokers are likely to call for more margin from their clients than they are required to provide to the clearing house.

Margin, minus any loss incurred, is returned when a position is closed or a contract reaches delivery.

Example
An organization buys 10 September eurodollar futures through its broker at a price of 93.60. The initial margin payment required was $7,500. In the next few weeks the price of the future dropped, and variation margin of $2,500 was called to cover losses on the (long) position. The position eventually was closed by selling 10 September contracts at 93.52.

Analysis
The loss per contract on the futures transactions has been:

Purchase price	93.60
Closing out price	93.52
Loss per contract	0.08

The loss is 8 ticks per contract.

For 10 contracts, the total loss therefore is:

$(8 x $25 x 10 contracts) = $2,000.

A summary of the cash movements is:

	$
Initial margin paid	7,500
Variation margin paid	2,500
	10,000
Loss on position	-2,000
Money returned to client	8,000

Marking-to-Market and Margin Calls

The process of marking-to-market at the close of each trading day is an integral part of the margin system.

At the close of trading each day, the clearing house calculates the day's gains or losses on the open positions of its members, revaluing their positions to closing prices (the exchange's daily settlement prices).

The gain or loss on each member's position that day is used to assess how much margin is now required. Variation margin might be called where losses have been incurred on the day. Surplus margin can be withdrawn (where a member's positions have made gains).

Example

An organization sells 10 March short sterling futures at a price of 94.70. The initial margin payable is £500 per contract. During the next six trading days, the daily settlement price was:

Day	Daily sett. price
1	94.75
2	94.78
3	94.71
4	94.66
5	94.64
6	94.73

Analysis

The broker will mark the client's position to market at the end of each day. Suppose the margin level must be maintained at a minimum of £5,000 until the position is closed, and suppose also that the client keeps any cumulative gains on the position in the account. The client's account might show the following transactions, in pounds sterling.

Note

The client has a short position, and so gains from a fall in the future's price and loses when the price rises.

Day	**Price change (ticks)**	**Value per tick**	**Gain/ loss in the day (10 contracts)**	**Cumul. gain/ loss**	**Variation margin call**	**Closing balance on account**
1	+ 5	12.50	- 625	- 625	+ 625	5,000
2	+ 3	12.50	- 375	- 1,000	+ 375	5,000
3	- 7	12.50	+ 875	- 125	- 875	5,000
4	- 5	12.50	+ 625	+ 500	- 125	5,500
5	- 2	12.50	+ 250	+ 750	-	5,750
6	+ 9	12.50	- 1,125	- 375	+ 375	5,000

In this example, the client paid variation margin after marking-to-market on Days 1 and 2, to cover the losses on the position on those days. Gains were recorded on the position for Days 3, 4 and 5: in this example, the client took back the variation margin that had been paid (£1,000), but the cumulative overall gain on the position was retained in the account. At the end of Day 6, another variation margin call is required, because the position has gone into an overall loss position again.

The example might illustrate that for organizations using futures regularly, the management of margin positions is a continual daily task.

Conclusion

This chapter has explained the trading system for futures, the role of the clearing house and the system of margins for providing protection against counterparty risk.

The next chapter explains closing positions, and settlement for positions that are kept open until delivery.

8

Closing Positions. Delivery

Closing a Position

Most futures positions are closed before delivery day. A position is closed simply by reversing the original transaction.

For example, an organization that has purchased 15 June US Treasury bond futures can close this position by selling 15 June futures at any time up to delivery day. There will be an overall gain or loss on the purchase and subsequent sale.

Similarly, an organization that has a short position of 20 March euribor futures can close this position at any time up to delivery by purchasing 20 March euribor futures, giving an overall gain or loss on the transactions.

The **gain or loss** is the difference between the original purchase price and closing sale price, or the original sale price and closing purchase price. The gain or loss in ticks per contract is multiplied by the value per tick and by the number of contracts. The gain is received or the loss is paid through cash settlement.

The **amount of cash receivable** when a position is closed is:

	Initial margin paid
Plus:	Variation margins paid (if any)
Plus:	Gain on the transactions, or
Minus:	Loss on the position
Minus:	Any cash withdrawals already made

Example

An organization sold 15 December euribor futures at 94.73 and paid its broker an initial margin of €6,000. The price of the future subsequently rose. The rise in price meant a loss for the seller of futures (someone with a short position) and variation margin calls of €2,700 were made.

On 4 December, the organization closed its position by purchasing 15 December futures at 94.79.

Analysis
There is an overall loss on the transactions:

Sell at	94.73
Purchase to close at	94.79
Loss per contract	0.06

The loss per contract is 0.06, 12 ticks. The value per tick is €12.50, therefore the total loss on the position is:

€12.50 x 12 ticks x 15 contracts = €2,250.

The cash returnable to the organization on closing the position is as follows:

	€
Initial margin	6,000
Variation margin payments	2,700
Less: Loss on transactions	- 2,250
Less: Cash already withdrawn	0
	6,450

Having made a loss on its short position, the organization receives back the margin payments it has made, minus the loss incurred.

Further example
A clearing member of the futures exchange has two clients, X and Y, who both make transactions in June Treasury bond futures.

- X bought 20 contracts at 93 – 04
- Y sold 15 contracts at 93 – 02

X and Y each pay initial margin to their broker, the clearing member, who is also required to pay some initial margin to the clearing house of the exchange. Suppose the initial margin payable by X is $10,000 and the initial margin payable by Y is $7,500.

The exchange clearing house will monitor the position of the clearing member through a daily marking-to-market process. Similarly, the clearing member will mark-to-market each day the positions of its clients X and Y. Where appropriate, variation margin calls will be made.

Suppose that X and Y both decide to close their position on the same day. X sells 20 June Treasury bond futures at 92–22 and Y buys 15 futures at the same price, 92–22.

Prices for US Treasury bond futures are quoted in 32nds, so the gain or loss per contract for X and Y is:

	X		Y
Buy at	93 – 04	Sell at	93 – 02
Sell to close at	92 – 22	Buy to close at	92 – 22
Loss per contract	14	Gain per contract	12

The loss made by X, at $31.25 per tick for 20 contracts, is:

$(31.25 x 14 x 20) = $8,750.

The gain made by Y, at $31.25 per tick for 15 contracts, is:

$(31.25 x 12 x 15) = $5,625.

Assuming that X paid variation margin to cover its losses and that Y made no cash withdrawals before closing its position, the cash returnable by the broker to each client on closing their positions is:

	X	Y
	$	$
Initial margin	10,000	7,500
Variation margin	8,750	
Gain		5,625
Loss	- 8,750	
Cash returnable	10,000	13,125

Why Are Positions Closed Before Delivery?

Positions in futures normally are closed before delivery.

- There are only a few delivery days in the year for futures contracts. Closing a position early, before delivery, gives the position holder **flexibility** in the choice of dates. If an organization is using interest-rate futures to hedge an exposure to interest-rate risk, closing a position can be made to match the timing of a short-term loan or deposit, or the date of another financial instrument, such as the notional loan period for an FRA.
- Organizations or individuals that trade in futures for speculative purposes will close their positions at a time of their own choosing, to realize a gain on their position or to limit any loss.

Delivery

Positions that are kept open to delivery day must be settled. There is a last day for trading in each contract, and a latest time on the last trading day, one or two days before the delivery day. Positions that are still open after this cut-off time will be settled on delivery.

- Short-term interest rate futures are cash-settled.
- Most bond futures are settled by physical delivery.

As counterparty to every transaction, the clearing house is in a position to ensure that all positions are properly settled.

Delivery by Cash Settlement

A contract where delivery is by cash settlement is known as a contract for difference. The seller does not deliver the underlying traded item to the buyer in exchange for payment at the agreed price. Instead, there is a cash payment in settlement, equal to the amount of the gain or loss on the position.

The delivery by cash settlement of futures contracts is settlement between:

- a buyer (holder of a long position) and the clearing house, or
- a seller (holder of a short position) and the clearing house.

Similarly, there is delivery by cash settlement for the clients of clearing house members.

The gain or loss on a position, for the purpose of delivery by cash settlement, is the difference between:

- the price at which the futures were bought or sold, to establish the open position, and
- the exchange delivery settlement price for the contract.

For example, the exchange delivery settlement price for the LIFFE-traded euribor contract is the European Bankers Federation Euribor Offered Rate (EBF Euribor), for three-month deposits as at 11.00 a.m. Brussels time on the last trading day for the contract. Delivery day is the day following the last trading day.

Cash settlement is carried out in a similar way to closing a position before delivery. Settlement is with the clearing house, and the clearing member receives back:

	Initial margin paid
Plus:	Variation margins paid (if any)
Plus:	Gain on the position at settlement, or
Minus:	Loss on the position at settlement
Minus:	Any cash withdrawals already made

A similar method of settlement of positions applies to the clients of clearing members, in settlement with the clearing member.

Example

An organization buys 25 December three-month eurodollar futures at a price of 93.68. The initial margin paid was $12,500.

Subsequently the price of the December contract falls, and the organization has to make variation margin (performance bond) payments of $6,250 to cover the losses on the position.

The position is kept open to delivery, and the exchange delivery settlement price is 93.61.

Analysis
There is a loss on delivery, as follows:

Bought at	93.68
EDSP	93.61
Loss per contract	0.07

The loss is 7 ticks per contract. At a value of $25 per tick, the total loss is:

$(7 ticks x $25 x 25 contracts) = $4,375

On delivery day, the cash returned to the organization will be:

	$
Initial margin	12,500
Variation margin payments	6,250
Less: Loss on transactions	- 4,375
Less: Cash already withdrawn	0
	14,375

Physical Delivery (Bond Futures)
Most positions in bond futures are closed before delivery. However, positions that are kept open to delivery are settled by physical delivery of bonds by a seller to a buyer. A seller delivers a quantity of actual bonds to a buyer, and the buyer pays for them.

An exception to the general rule that bond futures are settled by physical delivery is the LIFFE-traded Japanese government bond future, for which there is cash settlement on delivery.

There are several practical problems with settlement by physical delivery of bonds:

- the underlying bonds are notional bonds, not actual bonds
- the notional bonds pay a specified fixed coupon rate of interest that might be a different coupon to the interest rate paid on comparable actual bond issues
- with any actual bonds delivered by the seller of the futures, there will be accrued interest
- the seller's contract is with the clearing house, and the buyer's contract is with the clearing house: so how does a seller deliver bonds to a buyer?
- What is the price payable for the actual bonds on delivery?

Each of these issues will be considered in turn.

The Underlying Bonds are Notional Bonds: Choosing Actual Bonds to Deliver

The underlying bonds for a futures contract are notional bonds, not actual bonds. The exchange authorities therefore must identify one or more actual bond issues whose bonds would be acceptable for the purpose of settlement by physical delivery.

The exchange provides a list, for each contract delivery date, of actual bonds that will be acceptable for the settlement of the bond futures contract.

As examples:

- for the long gilt contract (LIFFE), the exchange authorities will select actual bond issues that have a remaining term to redemption of between 8.75 years and 13 years for the entire issue, and that are fixed-interest bonds with interest payable half-yearly.
- The five-year eurobond future (Matif) provides for the delivery of either French government securities (OATs or BTANs) or German government securities (Bunds or Bobls) with remaining terms to maturity of between 3.5 and 5.5 years.

The Coupon Rate of Interest: Adjustment Factors

The market value of bonds depends on several factors. Two major factors are:

- the rate of interest (coupon) receivable on the bond, and
- the remaining period of time to maturity, when the bonds will be redeemed.

The actual bond issues selected by the futures exchange authorities will differ from each other and will differ from the notional bonds in the futures contract in both of these respects. The coupon varies between bond issues, and the maturity dates of bond issues also will differ, although they all will lie within the range for the number of years to maturity given in the specifications for the bond future.

To bring the valuation of actual bond issues into line with the notional bonds in the future contract, an adjustment factor is applied.

Suppose the notional bonds for a bond future have a nominal value of €100,000, and some actual bonds are listed as acceptable for the purpose of physical delivery to settle the futures contracts:

- If these actual bonds are given an adjustment factor of 1.05 for example, the price payable by the buyer will be multiplied by this factor in arriving at the actual price payable.
- The adjustment factor might be less than 1.0. If actual bonds have an adjustment factor of 0.95, the price payable by the buyer will be multiplied by this factor in arriving at the actual price payable.

Adjustment factors are given to a number of decimal places.

The application of adjustment factors is illustrated in a later example.

Cheapest to Deliver

For a variety of reasons, such as the conversion factors applied to each actual bond issue, and slight differences between the futures market price and the cash market prices for bonds, one actual issue of bonds always will be cheapest to deliver. On physical delivery, the buyer should expect to receive these cheapest-to-deliver bonds, and pay the appropriate price. However, if there is an insufficient supply of the cheapest-to-deliver bonds in the market, the seller will have to deliver an alternative.

Accrued Interest

For actual bonds, there will be interest accrued as at the delivery date for the futures contract.

Accrued interest is interest payable on the bonds that has built up over time since the previous interest payment date, but has not yet been paid out to bondholders.

Example

The six-monthly interest for an issue of 6% gilts, UK government bonds, is paid in April and October each year. This gilts issue can be used to settle the September gilt futures contract.

If these gilts are used by a seller to settle a short position in the September futures contract, the bonds delivered to the buyer will have accrued interest from the previous interest payment date in April up to the delivery day for the bond future in September. This will represent interest for a period of about five months. The buyer will receive the bonds in September, and one month later, in October, will receive interest for a full six-month period from April.

Interest accrued up to the delivery day for the futures must be paid by the buyer. The purchase price excluding accrued interest is called the clean price for the bonds. The price payable inclusive of the accrued interest is known as the dirty price for the bonds.

Matching Seller with Buyer

When transactions are made on a futures exchange, the clearing house becomes the counterparty to every buyer and seller. However, the clearing house will not want to take delivery of bonds from sellers: it is not in the business of trading bonds. Therefore it nominates buyers with open positions, and calls on them to take the bonds in settlement of their position on delivery day.

The total number of contracts for which there are long positions must always must be equal to the number of contracts for which there are short positions. In this way it will be possible to identify a buyer, the holder of a long position, who will be required to take delivery of bonds from a seller.

What is the Settlement Price?

The buyers and sellers who are matched for the purpose of physical delivery of bonds almost certainly will not have made their original transactions in futures together. The seller will have sold futures at one price and the buyer will have bought futures at a different price. The settlement price therefore cannot be the price at which the original transactions were made.

The price payable by the buyer is based on the exchange delivery settlement price for the contract.

The full price payable is:

Nominal value of the bonds
Priced at the Exchange Delivery Settlement Price
Multiplied by the Adjustment Factor for the actual bonds used to deliver
Equals the Clean Price payable for the bonds

Add Accrued Interest
Equals the full price (Dirty Price) payable for the bonds

The Exchange Delivery Settlement Price is defined in the contract specifications. For the LIFFE-traded long gilt contract, for example, it is determined by the exchange as the price for the notional bonds as at 11.00 a.m. two business days prior to settlement day that is also the time of last trading in the contract.

Gains or Losses on Positions

The buyer must pay a price for the delivered bonds based on the exchange delivery settlement price, not the price at which he bought the futures originally. Similarly, the seller will receive a price for delivering actual bonds, based on the exchange delivery settlement price, not the actual price at which he sold the futures.

The buyer and the seller will make a gain or a loss on their futures transactions, equal to the difference at which they bought or sold the futures and the exchange delivery settlement price.

The seller's and the buyer's gain or loss is cash-settled through the clearing house of the exchange. Similarly, clients of clearing members will cash-settle their gains or losses on delivery day with the clearing member.

Example
An organization holds a short position in March Euro Bund futures and wishes to settle by physical delivery. The organization bought 10 Bund futures in January at 101.62.

The Exchange delivery Settlement Price in March is 101.50.

The cheapest-to-deliver actual bonds have a conversion factor of 1.00738591.

Accrued interest on the bonds to delivery date for the futures contract in March is 0.018, i.e. €1.08 per €100 nominal value of bonds.

The exchange identifies a buyer to take physical delivery of the bonds. This buyer bought 10 March contracts at a price of 101.85.

Euro Bund futures are for notional Bunds with a nominal value of €100,000.

Analysis
The Exchange Delivery Settlement Price is 101.50.

The nominal value of the notional bonds for one future contract is €100,000.

The conversion factor is 1.00738591.

The seller will deliver €100,000 (nominal value) of the cheapest-to-deliver bonds, for each futures contract settled.

The clean price paid for each €100,000 (nominal value) will be:

€100,000 x (101.50/100) x 1.00738591

= €102,249.66.

The dirty price includes accrued interest that for €100,000 (nominal value) is €1,800 (100,000 x 0.018).

The full price paid for each €100,000 actual bonds, per contract, is:

	Price payable per contract
	€
Clean price	102,249.66
Accrued interest	1,800.00
Full price	104,049.66

For 10 contracts the full price receivable for delivering €1,000,000 (nominal value) of actual bonds is €1,040,496.60.

The seller has made a gain on his futures transactions:

Sold at	101.62
EDSP	101.50
Gain per contract	0.12

The gain is 12 ticks per contract, and at €10 per tick for 10 contracts, the total gain is: €(12 x 10 x 10) = €1,200.

This will be receivable by the seller in cash through his margin account.

The buyer has made a loss on his futures trading:

Bought at	101.85
EDSP	101.50
Loss per contract	0.35

The loss is 35 ticks per contract, and at €10 per tick for 10 contracts, the total loss is: €(35 x 10 x 10) = €3,500.

This will be paid through the margin account (in variation margin).

9

Using Interest-Rate Futures

Interest-rate futures can be used for:

- hedging exposures to interest-rate risk
- speculating on changes in interest rates
- arbitrage, when opportunities arise.

Hedging Exposures to Interest-Rate Risk

Interest-rate risk is the risk of incurring losses through adverse movements in interest rates. An organization that borrows short-term or at a variable rate of interest is exposed to the risk of higher short-term interest rates. A depositor or investor in short-term funds is exposed to the risk of falling short-term interest yields. Bond investors are exposed to the risk of a rise in bond yields in the markets, and a consequent drop in bond prices.

Interest-rate futures can be used to hedge exposures to interest-rate risk.

- Short-term interest-rate futures can be used to lock in an interest rate for future short-term borrowing or investing.
- Bond futures can be used to protect a bond investor against the rise of rising yields and falling bond prices. They also can be used by someone who plans to make a bond investment in the near future, as a hedge against the risk of falling yields and rising bond prices in the period to making the investment.

Hedge required	How to use interest-rate futures
Lock in an effective interest rate for future short-term borrowing	Sell STIRs
Lock in an effective interest rate for future short-term investing	Buy STIRs
Obtain a hedge against the risk of falling bond prices	Sell bond futures
Obtain a hedge against the risk of rising bond prices	Buy bond futures

Note that:

- a hedge against the risk of losses or higher costs from higher interest rates is obtained by selling interest-rate futures
- a hedge against the risk of losses from lower interest rates is obtained by buying interest-rate futures.

The period of time for which futures can provide a hedge depends on the availability of futures with more distant delivery dates. In practise, the most heavily traded contracts are those with the nearest delivery dates. This suggests that hedging with futures has a relatively short-term planning horizon.

- Most bond futures are available only for trading for the next two, three or four delivery dates, i.e. up to about one year ahead.
- Some short-term interest-rate futures are available for delivery dates up to about five years ahead, although trading is thin in these long-dated contracts.

Short-Term Borrowing and Using Futures as a Hedge

The most commonly used STIR futures are contracts where the underlying item is a notional deposit of three months. STIRs therefore can be used to hedge the risk of higher borrowing costs for organizations

- expecting to borrow for a three-month term in the near future
- borrowing at a floating rate, with three-monthly rollover dates for interest.

STIRs also can be used to hedge against the risk of higher interest rates for short-term borrowing periods of more or less than three months. This is explained later.

Hedging with STIRs locks in a borrowing cost now for the future borrowing period.

STIR futures contracts should be priced in the market to reflect market expectations of what interest rates will be on the delivery day for the contract. June eurodollar futures, for example, should be traded at a price that reflects market expectations of what the three-month dollar interest rate will be in June. Changes in market expectations about what the interest rate will be should result in a change in the futures price.

An organization can sell STIR futures to lock in an interest cost for a future short-term borrowing. Hedging with STIRs works as follows:

- The organization sells STIR futures now. A seller of STIR futures is undertaking to provide the buyer with a notional deposit at a future date, and to pay a fixed rate of interest on that deposit. The rate of interest is fixed by the price at which the futures are sold.
- Selling STIR futures locks in an interest-rate level for the benchmark rate of interest the three-month rate for dollar LIBOR, sterling LIBOR or the euribor rate, etc.
- The organization will borrow at whatever the current interest rate happens to be at the time the loan is arranged.
- The organization will close its futures position to coincide with the start of the borrowing period.
- If interest rates were to rise between the time when the futures position was opened and the start of the borrowing period, the

organization's borrowing cost will be higher, but these higher costs will be offset by a gain on the futures transactions. Subtracting the gain on the futures trading from the actual interest cost for the borrowing, gives a net effective borrowing cost equivalent to the interest-rate cost that was locked in by selling the futures.

- If interest rates were to have fallen between the time the futures position was opened and the start of the borrowing period, the organization's borrowing cost will be lower. However, these lower interest costs will be offset by a loss on the futures transactions. Adding the loss on the futures trading to the actual interest cost for the borrowing, gives a gross effective borrowing cost equivalent to the interest-rate cost that was locked in by selling the futures.

Using STIRs to hedge short-term interest-rate exposures therefore locks in a borrowing cost, regardless of whether interest rates subsequently rise or fall.

Selling STIRs to Lock in a Future Borrowing Cost of X%

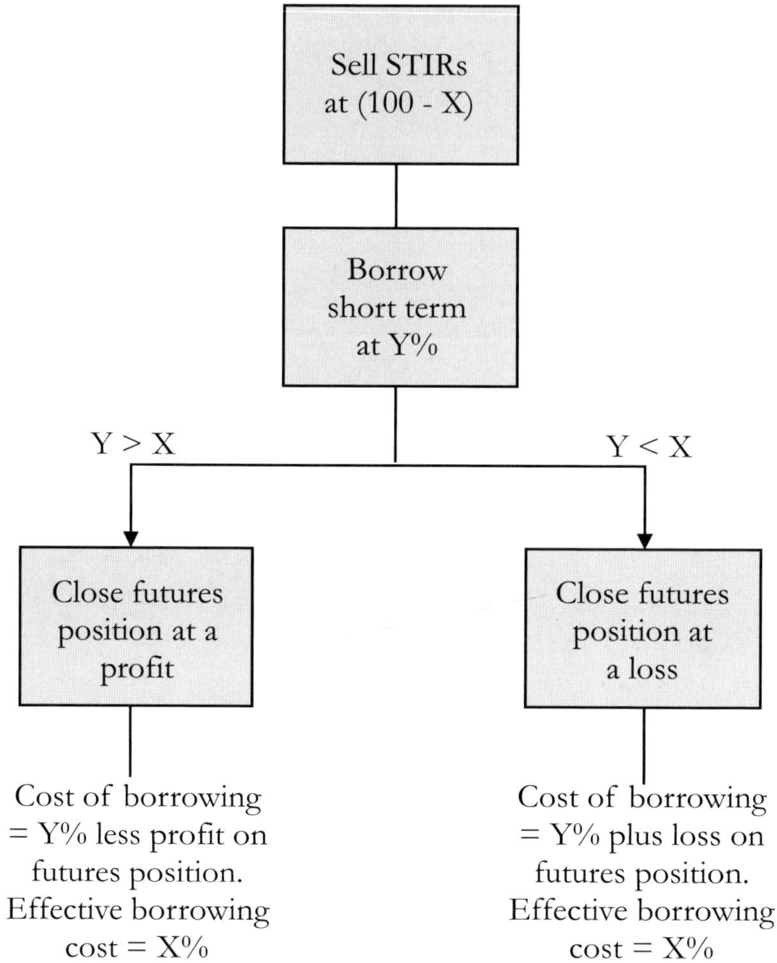

Example

An organization expects to borrow €20 million for three months from early September. It will borrow at the EBF euribor rate plus 25 basis points (0.25%).

The organization wishes to hedge the exposure to a rise in the euribor rate before September, therefore it sells 20 September euribor futures at a price of 95.25.

The interest rate shown by this price is 4.75% (100 – 95.25). Selling the futures will lock in a borrowing rate of 4.75% plus 25 basis points, i.e. 5.00%, for the organization. This is the effective interest rate at which it will be able to borrow the €20 million in September.

Analysis

Outcome 1

Suppose that in September, when the organization borrows the €20 million, the three-month euribor rate is higher than 4.75%. Suppose that it is 5.20%.

The organization will close its futures position by purchasing 20 September futures. The price paid will be in the region of 94.80 that is 100 minus the current euribor rate of 5.20. Let us suppose that the organization buys the futures for 94.80.

There will be a gain on closing the futures position.

Sold futures at	95.25
Bought to close position at	94.80
Gain per contract	0.45

The gain is 0.45, or 90 ticks. At €12.50 per tick, for 20 contracts, the total gain on the futures transactions is: €(90 x 12.50 x 20) = €22,500.

The organization will borrow €20 million at the euribor rate plus 0.25%, i.e. at 5.45%. The interest cost for the three-month period (91 days) will be:

€20,000,000 x 0.0545 x 91/360 = €275,528.

Subtracting the gain of €22,500 on the futures transactions from this interest cost gives a net effective interest cost of €253,028.

The effective euribor interest rate for the three-month period for the organization, allowing for its hedge with futures, is:

(253,028/20,000,000) x (360/91) = 0.0500, or 5.00%.

This is the effective interest rate that was locked in for the borrowing by the original sale of the futures.

The effect of the hedge can be summarized as follows:

Borrow at	5.45%
Gain on futures (points)	-0.45%
Effective borrowing cost	5.00%

Outcome 2

Suppose instead that in September, when the organization borrows the €20 million, the euribor rate is lower than 4.75%. Suppose it is 4.40%. The organization will borrow the funds at euribor plus 25 basis points, i.e. at 4.65%.

It will close its futures position by purchasing 20 September contracts. The price paid will be in the region of 95.60 (100 – 4.40). Let's suppose that this is the actual price paid for the contracts.

There will be a loss on the futures transactions.

Sold futures at	95.25
Bought to close position at	95.60
Loss per contract	0.35

The loss is 0.35, or 70 ticks. At €12.50 per tick, for 20 contracts, the total loss on the futures transactions is: €(70 x 12.50 x 20) = €17,500.

The organization will borrow €20 million at the euribor rate plus 0.25%, i.e. at 4.65 %. The interest cost for the three-month period (91 days) will be:

€20,000,000 x 0.0465 x 91/360 = €235,083.

Adding the loss of €17,500 on the futures transactions to this interest cost gives a gross effective interest cost of €252,583.

The effective interest rate for the three-month period for the organization, allowing for its hedge with futures, is:

(252,583/20,000,000) x (360/91) = 0.050, or 5.00%.

This is the effective interest rate that was locked in for the borrowing by the original sale of the futures.

The effect of the hedge can be summarized as follows:

Borrow at	4.65%
Loss on futures (points)	+0.35%
Effective borrowing cost	5.00%

Using futures to lock in an effective borrowing cost means that the borrower is protected against the risk of higher interest rates before the start of the borrowing period. However, the borrower will be unable to take advantage of any fall in interest rates, because lower borrowing costs will be offset by a loss on futures transactions.

Short-Term Investing and Hedging with Futures

An organization can use STIRs to lock in an effective investment yield from future short-term investments. Locking in an effective yield on an investment or deposit is similar in concept to locking in an effective interest cost on short-term borrowing. The only difference is that a hedge is created by purchasing futures to open a long position, and to close the position subsequently by selling futures.

Example
An organization, attracted by relatively high investment yields on short-term sterling investments, intends to invest £15 million in November for three months, and it expects to earn a yield of sterling LIBOR minus 20 basis points (0.20%) on its investment.

Concerned about the possibility of a fall in interest rates between now and November, it wishes to lock in an investment yield using short sterling futures. Therefore it buys 30 December short sterling futures (£500,000 per contract).

Suppose the price paid for the futures is 93.06, this reflects an interest rate of 6.94% (100 – 93.06). Buying the futures at this price locks in an investment yield for the organization of 6.94% minus 20 basis points, i.e. 6.74 %.

Analysis

Outcome 1

Suppose that in November, the three-month sterling LIBOR rate is lower than 6.94%. Suppose it is 6.42%. The organization will invest the £15 million at LIBOR minus 20 basis points, i.e. at 6.22%.

It will close its futures position by selling 20 December short sterling futures. The price obtained will be in the region of 93.58 (100 – 6.42). Let's suppose that this is the actual price obtained for selling the futures.

There is a gain on the futures transactions:

Bought futures at	93.06
Sold to close position at	93.58
Gain per contract	0.52

The gain is 52 ticks. At £12.50 per tick, for 30 contracts, the total gain on the futures transactions is: £(52 x 12.50 x 30) = £19,500.

The organization will invest £15 million at the sterling LIBOR rate minus 0.20%, i.e. at 6.22 %. The interest cost for the three-month period (92 days) will be:

£15,000,000 x 0.0622 x 92/365 = £235,167.

Adding the gain of £19,500 on the futures transactions to this interest income gives a gross effective investment income for the three months of £254,667.

The effective investment yield for the three-month period for the organization, allowing for its hedge with futures, is:

(254,667/15,000,000) x (365/92) = 0.0674, or 6.74%.

This is the effective investment yield that was locked in for the borrowing by the original purchase of the futures.

The effect of the hedge can be summarized as follows:

Invest at	6.22 %
Gain on futures (points)	0.52 %
Effective investment yield	6.74%

Outcome 2

Suppose that in November, three-month sterling LIBOR is higher than 6.94%, the rate implied by the futures price when the hedge was created. Suppose it was 7.25%. The organization will invest the £15 million in November at LIBOR minus 20 basis points, i.e. at 7.05%.

The organization will close its futures position at the same time, by selling 30 December futures contracts. The price will be around 92.75 (100 – 7.25). Let's suppose that the organization sells the futures at 92.75.

There will be a loss on closing the futures position, as follows:

Bought futures at	93.06
Sold to close position at	92.75
Loss per contract	0.31

The total loss, at £12.50 per tick for 31 ticks and 30 contracts, is

£(31 x 12.50 x 30) = £11,625.

The investment income from investing £15 million for three months (92 days) at 7.05% will be: £15,000,000 x 0.0705 x 92/365 =£266,548.

Subtracting the loss of £11,625 on the futures transactions gives a net effective investment income for the three-month period of £254,923.

This represents an effective net investment yield of:

(254,923/15,000,000) x (365/92) = 0.0674 or 6.74%.

This is the investment yield that was locked in by the original purchase of futures.

An organization that uses futures to hedge an exposure to the risk of falling interest rates will be unable to benefit from any subsequent rise in interest rates.

Using STIRs to Hedge Interest-Rate Risk for Different Borrowing Terms

Most short-term interest-rate futures are for notional deposits of three months. However, they can be used to hedge interest-rate risk where the borrowing term is less than or longer than three months.

To create the hedge, an adjustment should be made to the number of futures contracts. The adjustment is:

$$\text{Number of contracts required to hedge a three-month loan} \times \frac{\text{Actual term of loan}}{\text{3 months}}$$

For example, to hedge the exposure to a rise in the interest rate for a future six-month loan, an organization should sell twice the number of contracts (x 6/3) needed to hedge the interest-rate risk for a three-month loan.

The hedge is not perfect, because it is based on the assumption that any change in the general level of interest rates will be the same for all maturities. For example, if three-month interest rates were to rise by 50 points, it is assumed that the two-month, four-month and six-month interest rates etc. also would rise by 50 basis points. This assumption is not necessarily valid.

Example 1

An organization expects to borrow $30 million for six months in June at the dollar LIBOR rate, and it wishes to hedge its exposure to the risk of a rise in interest rates between now and then.

Each eurodollar future is for a notional three-month deposit of $1,000,000, so the organization therefore will sell 60 June eurodollar futures (30 x 6/3).

Analysis

Suppose that interest rates did rise by a full 1%, for both three-month and six-month dollar LIBOR, in the period to June.

- The organization will borrow at an interest rate 1% higher than anticipated, and the extra interest cost for the six months will be approximately $30,000,000 x 1% p.a. x 6/12, i.e. $150,000.
- The organization will close its futures position by purchasing

60 June eurodollar contracts. It will make a gain of 100 ticks (1%) per contract, and the gain on the futures transactions will be $25 per tick x 100 ticks x 60 contracts = $150,000.

The higher borrowing cost is offset by the gain on the futures transactions, meaning that the effective borrowing cost is the rate that was locked in by the original sale of the 60 futures contracts.

Example 2

An organization has a loan of £10 million with six-monthly rollover dates. It pays interest at the six-month sterling LIBOR rate, currently 6.20%.

It is concerned about the possibility of higher interest rates between now and the next rollover date for the loan, in June. It hedges its exposure by selling 40 short sterling contracts (£500,000 per contract) at 94.00. Although this might appear to lock in an interest rate of 6.00%, the actual interest rate locked in is 6.20%. This is because the six-month LIBOR rate, at 6.20%, is 0.20% above the three-month interest rate in the futures price.

By the time the next rollover date for the loan arrives, interest rates have risen by 0.75%. The six-month sterling LIBOR rate is now 6.95%. The futures price has fallen by 0.75, and the organization closes its position by purchasing 40 June contracts at 93.25.

Analysis

The organization will pay interest at 6.95% for the next six months and the interest payable will be (183 days):

£10 million x 0.0695 x 183/365 = £348,452.

The gain on the futures position will be:

Sold futures at	94.00
Bought to close position at	93.25
Gain per contract (ticks)	0.75

At £12.50 per tick for 40 contracts, the total gain on the futures transactions is:

£(75 ticks x 12.50 x 40) = £37,500.

The net effective borrowing cost, subtracting the gain on the futures transactions from the actual interest payable, is £310,952.

This is an effective interest cost for the six-month period of:

(310,952/10,000,000) x (365/183) = 0.062, i.e. 6.2%.

This is the interest rate that was locked in by selling the futures.

The hedge can be summarized as follows:

Rise in interest rate	+ 0.75 %
Reduction in effective interest rate from futures transactions	- 0.75 %
Change in effective interest cost	Nil

Basis Risk

STIRs do not provide a perfect hedge against short-term interest rate risk. The main reason for this is basis risk.

Basis is the difference between the spot price or cash market price for an item and the futures price for the same item. For short-term interest rates, basis is the difference between the actual money-market interest rates and the interest rate in the futures price.

Basis might be measured as a percentage amount or proportion, usually for the futures contract with the nearest delivery date.

$$\text{Basis} = \frac{\text{Cash price minus futures price}}{\text{Futures price}}$$

Basis exists because demand-and-supply conditions differ between the cash markets and the futures markets. For example, speculative activity in the futures market could push the futures price above or below the comparable cash market/money-market price.

Where the cash market price and the futures market price differ, using

STIRs to hedge an interest-rate exposure will provide only an imperfect hedge, because it will not lock in an exact interest rate.

Example

An organization expects to borrow $20 million for three months in May at the dollar LIBOR rate, and wishes to use futures to lock in a borrowing cost. It sells 20 June eurodollar futures at a price of 94.00. The organization should expect to have locked in an interest rate for the borrowing of 6.00% (100 – 94.00)

Suppose that when the organization borrows the $20 million in May, it does so at the prevailing three-month dollar LIBOR rate of 6.25%. It closes its futures position by purchasing 20 June eurodollar futures, and the price it obtains is 93.85. The futures price shows an interest rate of 6.15%.

The gain on closing the futures position is 15 points:

Sold futures at	94.00
Bought to close position at	93.85
Gain per contract	0.15

The organization's effective borrowing cost is not the 6.00% it thought it had locked in, but 6.10%.

Borrow at	6.25 %
Gain on futures	- 0.15 %
Net effective borrowing cost	6.10 %

In this example the effective borrowing cost was not 6.00% because of the difference between the cash market price, i.e. the borrowing cost, for the borrowing that was 6.25%, and the interest rate implied in the futures price that was 6.15%.

Buying and Selling the Spread

On the last trading day for a futures contract, basis should be zero. If there were a difference between the futures price and the cash market price at this time, the opportunity would exist for arbitrage, i.e. making an immediate and certain profit from trading between the futures and the cash markets.

Basis can exist, however, in the period up to the last trading day for a futures contract, and it can fluctuate in size over time.

Speculators might trade in futures, hoping to profit from changes in the size of basis over time.

- Buying the spread means speculating on a narrowing of the basis over time. The speculator buys futures for a near delivery date and sells the same futures, but for a later delivery date.
- Selling the spread means speculating on a widening of the basis over time. The speculator sells futures for a near delivery date and buys the same futures, but for a later delivery date.

Example
In January, the three-month sterling LIBOR rate is 7.00%, and the price of March short sterling futures is 92.90 and the price of September short sterling futures is 92.85. Therefore the difference between the cash market price (in terms of futures prices, 93.00) and the futures price is 10 points for the March contract and 15 points for the September contract.

A speculator believes that the basis will widen between nearer-dated futures and further-dated futures and so buys March futures at 92.90 and sells September futures at 92.85.

In early February, the cash market price is 7.25% (92.75 in futures pricing terms), the price of the March contract is 92.70 and the price of the September contract is 92.60. The difference between the cash market price and the price of the March future is 5 points and the difference between the cash market price and the September future is 15 points. The basis has widened over time.

The speculator might close his/her positions by:

- selling March futures at 92.70 and
- buying September futures at 92.60.

March futures		
Buy at	92.90	
Sell to close position at	92.70	
Loss per contract		- 0.20
September futures		
Sell at	92.85	
Buy to close position at	92.60	
Gain per contract		+ 0.25
Net gain		0.05

The speculator has made a profit from the change in the relative size of the basis for the March and the September contracts. The actual interest rate is irrelevant to the earning of a profit that arises simply from the change in basis.

Stack Hedging and Strip Hedging

An organization might wish to hedge the interest-rate risk for a floating-rate loan with three-monthly rollover dates. It can use STIRs to hedge the exposure by means of either

- stack hedging or
- strip hedging.

Example

An organization has a loan of $10 million with three-monthly rollover dates, on 1 March, 1 June, 1 September and 1 December each year. The company wants to hedge the exposure to the risk of rising interest rates over the course of the next 12 months. It is now January.

Stack hedging

In order to stack hedge, the organization will create a new hedge for the next three-month period at each rollover date. In January, it will hedge the interest-rate risk for the period to March by selling 10 March eurodollar futures. In March, it will hedge the interest-rate risk to June by selling 10 June eurodollar futures. Subsequently it will sell

10 September futures in June and 10 December futures in September.

Strip hedging
To strip hedge, the organization will create a hedge now for the full period. It will do so by selling 10 March futures, 10 June futures, 10 September futures and 10 December futures in January. This will lock in interest rates for the next four rollover dates for the loan, although the interest rate will differ for each rollover date. This is because the prices in January of the March, June, September and December contracts will not be the same.

Hedging with Bond Futures

The price of bonds rises or falls in response to changes in interest rates in the bond markets. If market yields rise, bond prices fall. Lower market yields result in higher bond prices.

Bond investors might wish to hedge against the risk from changes in bond prices in the next few months, and can do this with bond futures.

- A bondholder can hedge against the risk of a fall in the value of his bond portfolio by selling bond futures. If bond yields rise and bond prices fall, the loss in value in the bond portfolio will be offset by a gain on the bond futures position.
- An investor expecting to invest in bonds in the near future can hedge against the risk of a fall in bond yields and a rise in bond prices by purchasing bond futures. If bond yields were to fall before the investment is made, the higher cost of acquiring the bonds would be offset by a profit on the futures position.

The hedge will provide a better fit for bond portfolios where the bonds in the portfolio are similar to the notional bonds underlying the bond futures. For example, a hedge with US Treasury bond futures will be better-suited to a portfolio of long-term US Treasury bonds than a portfolio of dollar-denominated corporate bonds.

However, bond futures can provide a hedge against interest-rate risk provided that the prices of the bonds in the portfolio respond to changes in market yields in a similar way to the bonds underlying the futures contracts. For example, investors in dollar-denominated eurobonds of highly rated companies can use US Treasury bond futures as a hedge against interest-rate risk, provided it can be assumed that the prices of the corporate bonds will respond to changes in market yields in the same way as the price of US Treasuries.

Example

An organization holds €50 million (nominal value) of long-term German government 5.375% bonds for which the current market price is 100.15, giving a yield of 5.35%. The organization is concerned about the risk of a rise in the market yield for these bonds. It has decided to use futures to provide a hedge against the risk of a fall in bond prices between now (May) and September.

The current price of the September Euro Bund future is 103.80.

Analysis

To create a hedge, the organization should sell September Euro Bund futures. Each future is for €100,000 (nominal value) of notional bonds, and therefore it should sell 500 contracts.

Suppose that bond yields do rise, and as a consequence the market price of the organization's Bunds falls by 50 points from 100.15 to 99.65.

The price of the Bund futures also will fall, and should do so by about 50 points. Suppose the price of the September future falls from 103.80 to 103.30.

The organization could close its futures position by purchasing 500 September contracts at 100.30, providing a gain of 50 points per contract on the futures transactions.

Loss in value of Bunds	(€50 million x 0.0050)	€250,000
Gain on futures	(500 contracts x 50 ticks x €10 per tick)	€250,000

The loss in value in the bond portfolio is offset by the gain on the futures transactions.

Speculation

Futures can be used to speculate. Speculators might hope to outguess the market by taking positions in futures. If prices move favorably, the futures positions can be closed at a profit.

An advantage of using futures for price speculation is the relatively low investment required to bet on relatively large amounts.

The investment required to speculate in futures is the initial margin payments plus variation margin to cover any losses. An initial margin of about $500 might be sufficient to buy or sell a eurodollar future, for which the underlying item is a notional deposit of $1,000,000. Similarly, a relatively small margin is needed to invest in bond futures where the underlying item is notional bonds with a nominal value of €100,000 or $100,000.

Example

A speculator expects the dollar LIBOR rate to rise in the near future. He/she can sell a eurodollar future and pay an initial margin. Suppose the margin paid is $500. Suppose also that the interest rate rises by 50 points (0.50%) and the price of the eurodollar future falls by 50 points.

The speculator can close his/her position by purchasing one future, and the gain will be (50 ticks at $25per tick) $1,250. This gain will have been made on an investment of $500, giving a return in this example of 250%.

If the speculator's gamble turned out to be wrong, and dollar interest rates fell rather than rose, he/she could control the subsequent losses by closing the position at any time.

Arbitrage Activity and Futures

Arbitrage is the buying and selling of related financial instruments or investments in order to make an immediate and certain profit from price discrepancies between different instruments or different markets. These price differences should be temporary because arbitrageurs will continue to exploit the opportunity for instant profit until market prices adjust and the price discrepancies disappear. These price adjustments should be quite rapid.

Who Uses Futures?

Interest-rate futures are used primarily by banks and other financial institutions. These have large amounts of financial assets and liabilities, and interest-rate futures are one instrument for managing financial risk.

Banks, for example, might use interest-rate futures to hedge the risk in their positions for loans and deposits, FRAs or interest-rate swaps. Investment institutions might use bond futures to hedge the price risk in their bond portfolios.

Advantages of using interest-rate futures	Disadvantages of using interest-rate futures
Gearing. Relatively large amounts can be hedged for a relatively small cash deposit (initial margin)	Hedging with futures locks in an interest rate. The hedger cannot benefit from any subsequent favorable movement in interest rates unlike a buyer of interest-rate options.
The futures markets are liquid, particularly for near delivery dates. Positions can be opened and closed with ease. Futures therefore are a flexible instrument to use.	Basis risk exists, and a hedge with futures might not be perfect.
Futures might be more convenient than over-the-counter instruments as a means of hedging interest-rate exposures.	Organizations that are not clearing members of the futures exchange must channel their transactions through a clearing member.
Futures are cheaper than some alternative hedging instruments, particularly interest-rate options.	The administrative effort of monitoring and managing futures positions and margin payments can be burdensome.

Glossary

Arbitrage
The simultaneous sale and purchase of identical or similar financial instruments for the purpose of making an immediate profit from a discrepancy in their prices (a mispricing of one of the instruments).

Ask
See Offer.

Bid
The price that a dealer is willing to pay for an instrument. For interest-rate futures, a dealer's bid price will be lower than his offer price. For FRAs, bid prices are higher than offer prices.

Bid-offer spread
The difference between a dealer's bid price and offer price.

Cash settlement
The settlement of a futures position on delivery day by means of a cash receipt or payment, rather than by means of physical delivery of the underlying item.

Clearing house
An organization that acts on behalf of a futures exchange and arranges for the settlement of contracts and margin requirements from clearing members.

Clearing member
A member of a futures exchange that is also a member of the clearing house of the exchange.

Closing a position
Terminating a long position by arranging an offsetting sale of futures or terminating a short position by arranging an offsetting purchase of futures.

Closing range
The range between the high and low prices during the short period designated as the official close of a trading session. The closing range is used by the exchange authorities to determine the daily settlement price for a contract.

Contract
A unit of trading for a future.

A transaction in futures between two parties, a buyer and seller, at an agreed price.

Contract for difference
A contract that is cash-settled rather than settled by physical delivery of the underlying item.

Contract month
The delivery month for a futures contract. Futures are traded for delivery in March, June, September and December for up to several years ahead. Most active trading in futures is in the nearest contract months.

Conversion factor
Used for the settlement of bond futures. This is a factor used to convert a quantity of notional bonds into an equivalent quantity of actual bonds.

Delivery
The delivery of the underlying instrument on delivery day for a contract, or the receipt or payment of cash in settlement of a futures contract (cash-settled contracts). Also referred to as Settlement.

Derivative
A financial instrument, such as a future, FRA or option, whose value is derived in part from the value or future price of an underlying

instrument. The value of short-term interest-rate futures is derived from the interest value of an underlying notional short-term money-market deposit. The value of an option on a future is derived from the value of the underlying future.

Exchange Delivery Settlement Price
The settlement price for a futures contract determined by the exchange authorities on the last trading day for the contract. Open positions in cash-settled contracts are settled on delivery day by comparing the contract price(s) for the futures and the Exchange Delivery Settlement Price.

Floor broker
A member of a futures exchange who executes orders for clearing members of the futures exchange or their customers, in return for a fee.

Floor trader
Also called a local. A member of the futures exchange who trades for his/her own account.

Forward/forward rate
An interest rate for a future interest period derived from two other interest rates. For example, the forward/forward rate for an interest period starting at the end of month 3 and ending at the end of month 6 (the 3 v 6 forward/forward rate) can be derived from the spot interest rates for three months and six months.

Forward-rate agreement (FRA)
An agreement to pay or receive interest on a notional loan or deposit at a fixed rate of interest in exchange for interest at a reference rate. The reference rate is determined on a fixing date just before settlement. FRAs can be described as single-period interest-rate swaps.

Hedge
A transaction or position that eliminates or reduces a financial risk. In the case of FRAs and interest-rate futures, a hedge involves buying or selling an FRA or futures, in anticipation of a cash market transaction at

a later date. A hedge usually involves taking an opposite position to the eventual cash market transaction.

Initial Performance Bond or Initial margin
An initial cash deposit payable by someone taking a position in futures. Initial margin is payable by a client to a broker, and by the broker to the clearing house of the exchange.

International Monetary Market (IMM)
Division of the Chicago Mercantile Exchange (CME) that specializes in financial futures.

Last trading day
The final day on which a futures contract can be traded for a given delivery day. For short-term interest-rate futures, this is the business day before the delivery day.

Local
See Floor broker.

Long position
A market position in futures where a quantity of the futures have been purchased. A state of being a net buyer of futures.

Maintenance margin
Also called maintenance performance bond. A part of the initial margin that must be kept in the customer's account at all times. If the balance on the account falls below the maintenance margin level because of losses on a futures position, a variation margin call or performance bond call will be made to restore the cash on deposit to the maintenance margin level.

Margin
Also called performance bond. Cash paid by a client to his broker, and by a broker to the clearing house of the exchange. Margin protects the broker against losses on the client's position and the exchange against losses on the broker's positions. Initial margin is paid when a futures

position is opened. Subsequently, additional variation margins might be required to cover losses on futures positions. Where gains are made on a futures position, cash can be withdrawn and the margin level reduced.

Margin call
Also known as a performance-bond call. A demand for an additional margin payment. See also Variation margin.

Marking to market
The daily adjustment of a customer's account by a broker and of a clearing member's account by the clearing house of the exchange. The positions of customers/clearing members are revalued to their current market value (the exchange's daily settlement price). The marking-to-market process is used to determine gains or losses during the day on futures positions, and the amount of any variation margin required.

Maximum price fluctuation
The maximum amount by which a futures price can change during a trading session. Maximum price fluctuations are imposed by futures exchanges in order to restrict price volatility.

Minimum price fluctuation
See Tick.

Offer
Also known as Ask. In the case of futures, a price at which a dealer is willing to sell a futures contract.

Offset
In the case of someone holding a long position in futures, selling futures. In the case of someone holding a short position in futures, buying futures. The offset reduces or eliminates the long or the short position. An offset that eliminates a position is referred to as closing the position.

Open interest
The total number of futures contracts for a given delivery date that have

not yet been eliminated by offset. A large open interest is an indication of a liquid market in the futures contract.

Option on a future
An instrument giving its buyer the right, but not the obligation, to buy (call option) or sell (put option) a futures contract at a specified price (the strike price) at any time up to the expiry date for the option that must be no later than the last trading day for the future.

Over-the-counter agreement
An agreement or contract arranged directly between two parties, where the specific terms of the contract are tailored to the requirements of one or both parties. An agreement that is not exchange-traded.

Position
An interest in futures. Someone who has bought futures and not offset them holds a long position. Someone who has sold futures and not offset them holds a short position.

Performance bond
See Margin.

Performance-bond call
See Margin call.

Physical delivery
Settlement of a futures contract whereby the seller delivers the underlying item to a buyer. Bond futures are settled by physical delivery.

Position risk
Market risk arising from holding a long position or a short position in an item.

Range
The high and low prices at which futures transactions are recorded within a specified time period.

Settlement price
A price decided by the exchange authorities to calculate gains or losses on futures positions. Settlement prices are determined at the end of each day (the daily settlement price) and finally on the last trading day for a contract (the Exchange Delivery Settlement Price).

Short position
A position of being a net seller of an instrument. A person holding a short position in futures has sold futures contracts and has not yet closed the position by making an offsetting purchase.

Speculator
Someone who trades in an item, hoping to profit from future movements in the market price.

A speculator trades in price risk.

Strip of FRAs
A series of FRAs bought or sold on the same date and for a series of successive interest-rate periods, for example 2 v 5, 5 v 8, 8 v 11 and 11 v 14 FRAs.

Swap
An interest-rate swap is an agreement to exchange interest payments on a notional amount of principal, at pre-determined payment dates for the duration of the agreement. One party might agree to pay interest at a fixed rate, and the other party might pay interest at a floating rate, determined before each payment date by reference to a benchmark rate of interest, such as LIBOR.

Tick
The minimum price movement in a futures contract.

Volume
The number of transactions in a futures contract in a specified period of time, usually one day. The purchase of futures by one party and the sale by the other party counts as one transaction.

Index

Notes

Notes

Notes

Notes